The Hair Commandments

Shalls and Shall Nots of Wigs, Weaves and Natural Hair

LaToya Johnson-Rainey
C. Nathaniel Brown

Atlanta, GA

Copyright © 2014 LaToya Johnson-Rainey and C. Nathaniel Brown All rights reserved. No part of this book may be reproduced or transmitted in any form or by any means, electronic or mechanical, including photocopy, recording, or by any information storage and retrieval system with the exception of a reviewer who may quote brief passages in a review to be printed in a blog, newspaper or magazine without written permission from the author. Address inquiries to: Expected End Entertainment, P.O. Box 1751, Mableton, GA 30126.
Published by Expected End Entertainment/EX3 Books
ExpectedEndEntertainment@gmail.com
www.EX3ent.com

Library of Congress Control Number: 2014918315
ISBN-10: 0988554550
ISBN-13: 978-0-9885545-5-9
Printed in the United States of America

Cover Images:
Model Lai-Ling Bernstein, Stephanie Eley/SEE Photography
The Bald Movement, Photographer: Ryan Eric
Models: Halaveshia, Nina, Nell, Angel, and Tanieka
Model: Akia Uwanda, Micheal Helms, Photographer
Model Tanesha Smart, Laretta Houston, Photographer

DEDICATION

LaToya: This book is dedicated to everyone who has ever had a rough start, grief, and discernment but got through it. You are appreciated!

Chuck: I dedicate this book to those who entrust me to help them Dream Bigger, Live Their Dreams and Impact Their World. The best is yet to come.

ACKNOWLEDGEMENTS

LaToya: A special thanks to my "Superman", my protector, my Boo Boo, my husband Dwayne Rainey. You are the best man I've ever known. To my Nana Josephine Mukwita and my best friend Erica Lowry, you both are strong and beautiful. Thanks for always being there! Also, thanks to all the strong and loving women in my family. You all make the world a better place. I love you all more than words can ever express.

Rest in God's loving care and please continue to look out for me my angels in heaven: my mother Sandy; my baby girl Brooklyn; my Great Grandmother Ila Mae; my Grandpa Sam, and my Uncle Wayne. I feel your love all the time.

I am thankful for God's grace that perseveres even when I don't deserve it.

Chuck: Special thanks to my wife Tarai Alexander, my children, Britt and Brad, and my grandson, Kyan for allowing me to be inspired, motivated and encouraged because of our love. My angels… Granny and Mom…
Much love to the best mother in the world, Ellen Brown.
Love to my dads, Tyrone and Tim.
To God be the glory!

CONTENTS

	Introduction	i
1	Wigs	1
2	How to Choose the Right Wig	4
3	How to Take Care of My Wig	32
4	Wigs Shalls and Shall Nots	34
5	Weaves	37
6	What are the Different Qualities	38
7	What Length to Choose	49
8	What are My Application Options	50
9	Weaves Shalls and Shall Nots	53
10	Natural Hair	55
11	The Big Chop	56
12	Texture Types	61

13	Natural Hair Care	67
14	Natural Hair Styles	70
15	Natural Hair Examples	72
16	Natural Shalls and Shall Nots	83
17	The Bald Movement	85
18	Healthier Hair with Giovan Lane	97
19	Ancient Secrets with Temeka Royster	107
20	Vitamins by Hairnamics with Kim Kearney	111
21	Stylists Soundoff	115
22	Wrap Up	125
23	Journal	127
24	About the Authors	131

INTRODUCTION

There is a battle that many women have with themselves daily. What should I do with my hair? Hair is at the forefront of how women appear whether it is for religious beliefs covering it for modesty or for a symbol of beauty. Hair is essential to the way we view our outer selves and it ultimately effects our confidence. Studies show that women are more productive when they feel good about their outer appearance and their hair is complimentary. When experiencing bad hair days, women tend to be sluggish, less productive, and in lower spirits. The symbolism of hair has made the beauty & hair industry a huge business that thrives even in a troubled economy. **Revenue from the U.S. hair care services industry is expected to exceed $58 billion by 2019.**

When faced with the challenge of hair styles, care, and treatment there are many options. Some women take pride in going natural, free of chemicals and enhancements, while others choose enhancements such as weaves and wigs. Of course there are pros and cons to any choice but no matter what you choose there are SHALLS & SHALL NOTS, DOS and DONTS. This book will answer some of the most popular questions as well as provide insight based on different vantage points: the distributor; the supplier; the stylist; the dermatologist; and the consumer. Through research, interviews, and trials, we compiled this information to save you precious time and money and ultimately help you make the best decisions as it relates to your hair care.

WIGS

One may choose to wear wigs for many reasons... convenience/fashion, medically-caused hair loss, or modesty.

People who enjoy the convenience of wigs find comfort in being able to put on a wig and have a complete style within minutes, sometimes seconds. They find wigs easier to maintain than their own hair and they are able to achieve a style or color without the commitment of involving their own hair. Some would like to wear a trendy haircut or perhaps they would like to go longer or fuller or just maybe wear a different color. This is the main reason why wigs are so popular with entertainers. You are able to experience hair versatility without damaging your natural hair.

Wigs are also an alternative when people experience medical hair loss, which can include diseases such as alopecia or loss as a result of chemotherapy.

Alopecia is a medical autoimmune condition that causes hair loss not only to the scalp but sometimes over the entire body. There are different types of alopecia with the most popular being alopecia areata and traction alopecia.

Alopecia areata usually starts in small, round, and smooth patches that spread and sometimes results in complete baldness. The hair follicles that are affected are tiny and prevent visible hair from growing beyond the skins surface. Some people only experience balding in patches and it may grow back within a year. In more serious cases called alopecia totalis all of the hair is lost on the scalp and may or may not grow back. Over 6.5 million people in the United States are affected by alopecia areata.

Traction alopecia is caused by damage of the hair

follicles and the dermal papilla. Constant pulling on the hair causes this condition that is most common in African-American and Japanese women because of some styles they choose that pull on the hair and cause tension. This includes the improper wear and care of braids, ponytails, and weaves. Over processing hair can also cause traction alopecia such as relaxers, hair dyes, and bleaching. If detected early, traction alopecia can be reversed. However, if not treated early enough it can cause permanent damage and balding to the scalp. If someone notices the symptoms of traction alopecia, they should consult dermatologist as soon as possible and opt for looser hairstyles.

Many people who suffer from alopecia experience emotional reactions. These feelings may include low self-esteem, sadness, embarrassment, self-blame, and loneliness. In some cases of alopecia, women are more likely to wear wigs daily and for long periods of time. Wigs are just one alternative as some people opt for more long-term fixes such graphing or high-end custom wigs. These alternatives may help build confidence and make a huge difference in someone's life.

People who experience hair loss such as that caused from chemotherapy or hair loss due to aging, stress, and heredity many times find comfort and increased confidence when finding the perfect wig. If someone knows that they are going to experience hair loss and would like a natural-looking wig, they should have a wig consultation prior to losing their hair. This will help the wig expert find the perfect match.

I. HOW TO CHOOSE THE RIGHT WIG?

Every wig is not for everyone. Selecting wigs that will work best for you takes a bit of knowledge, understanding, and decision making. Choosing the appropriate wig depends on face shape, cap size, hair type preference, cap construction, and color.

Model: Tanesha Smart   **Photographer:** Jeff Martin

THE HAIR COMMANDMENTS

Your face shape will help you find what style will best suit you. Choosing a wig that flatters your face shape will help the hairstyle look more natural. Look for styles that accentuate your positive attributes, while taking the attention away from areas that may cause an unbalanced look.

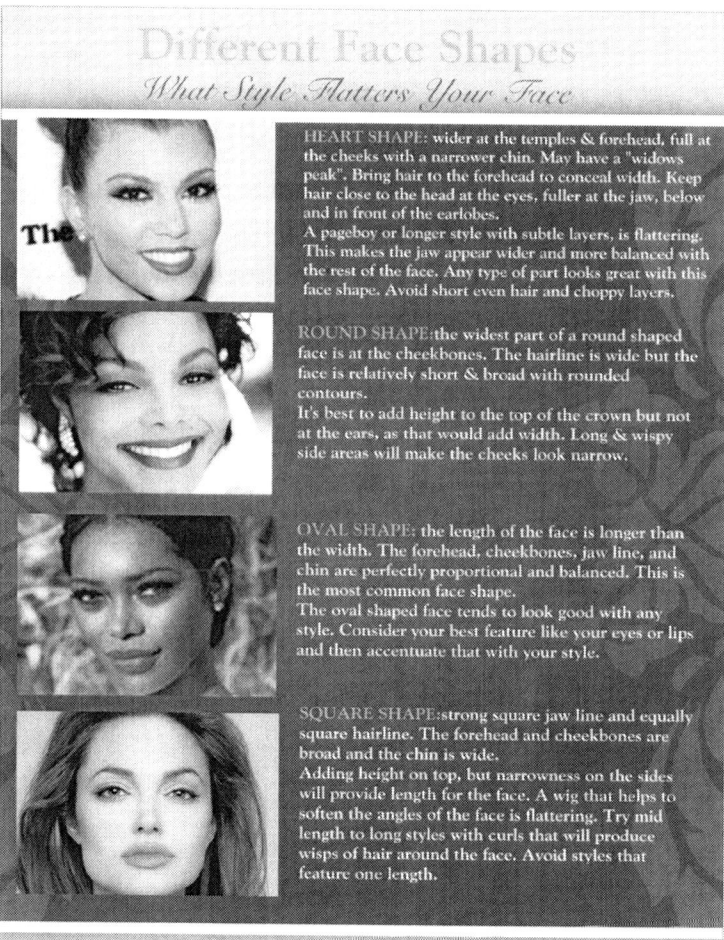

Different Face Shapes
What Style Flatters Your Face

HEART SHAPE: wider at the temples & forehead, full at the cheeks with a narrower chin. May have a "widows peak". Bring hair to the forehead to conceal width. Keep hair close to the head at the eyes, fuller at the jaw, below and in front of the earlobes.
A pageboy or longer style with subtle layers, is flattering. This makes the jaw appear wider and more balanced with the rest of the face. Any type of part looks great with this face shape. Avoid short even hair and choppy layers.

ROUND SHAPE: the widest part of a round shaped face is at the cheekbones. The hairline is wide but the face is relatively short & broad with rounded contours.
It's best to add height to the top of the crown but not at the ears, as that would add width. Long & wispy side areas will make the cheeks look narrow.

OVAL SHAPE: the length of the face is longer than the width. The forehead, cheekbones, jaw line, and chin are perfectly proportional and balanced. This is the most common face shape.
The oval shaped face tends to look good with any style. Consider your best feature like your eyes or lips and then accentuate that with your style.

SQUARE SHAPE: strong square jaw line and equally square hairline. The forehead and cheekbones are broad and the chin is wide.
Adding height on top, but narrowness on the sides will provide length for the face. A wig that helps to soften the angles of the face is flattering. Try mid length to long styles with curls that will produce wisps of hair around the face. Avoid styles that feature one length.

Choosing a wig that flatters your face shape will help the hairstyle look more natural. Look for styles that accentuate your positive attributes, while drawing attention away from areas that may cause an unbalanced look.

A. **Cap Size** – Finding the correct cap size is important for comfort as well as assuring a secure fit.

1. Most wigs only come in the average size which works for over 80% of clients. They take a few inches into consideration by adding adjustable straps that give or take about a 1/2 inch for a more secure fit. However, there are some designers that provide different petite and large cap size options. It is not uncommon for cancer treatment patients and other hair loss clients to need a petite size cap size. In addition, some clients have smaller than average or larger than average head sizes.

2. Please use a measuring tape and follow the instructions on the next page to determine your correct cap size. Be certain to measure the circumference of your head from the front hairline, behind the ear, to the nape of the neck, to the other ear and then back to the front hairline. After jotting down the results, consult the wig cap size chart to find your best fit.

THE HAIR COMMANDMENTS

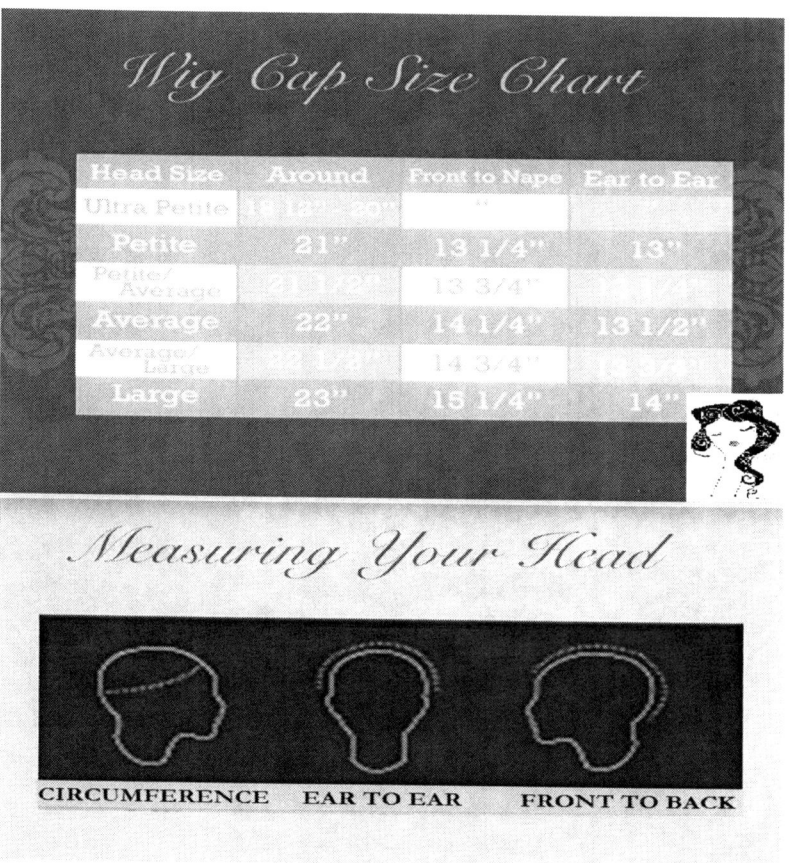

3. Please understand that sizes may vary depending on the brand and that every wig does not come in different cap sizes. When ordering, you will notice cap size options for the specific wigs that offer multiple choices.

B. **Hair Types: Synthetic, High Grade Heat-Resistant Synthetics, Human Blend, and Human Hair.**

1. Synthetic wigs are polymer and comprised of a variety of plastic fibers to appear like human hair. The wide array mix of fibers alter the quality of the wig. Lower grade synthetics are made from low grades of acrylic that is heated to create strands of hair-like fibers. They lack the movement and natural hair feel of human hair. These wigs are usually used for costumes or fashion wigs that are not worn daily. The price for these wigs can range from $10 to $50. Do not spend more than that for them because they are not worth it. A few brands that make this type of wig include It's A Wig, Vivica Fox, Motown Tress, and Revlon.

2. Higher grade synthetic wigs are also polymer but they are made with higher grades of acrylic, kanekalon, and other fiber that are more complexly blended. This gives the wig a more natural look and movement that can be created into a silky straight texture, curly texture, or kinky texture. They last longer than the low-grade synthetics and can be worn daily. These wigs usually come styled and the fibers allow the wig to maintain the style with little to no resetting. Even after

washing, the style usually remains in these wigs. Some brands ante up the grade by adding materials such futra that permits low-setting heat for further styling. These wigs are generally the easiest to maintain and the most moderately priced. However, the price range is widely gapped at $30 to $500. A few brands that specialize in these types of wigs include Raquel Welch, Gabor, Jon Reneau, and Rene' of Paris.

3. Human Hair Blended Wigs tend to offer the best of both worlds as they maintain their style and are a little easier to care of like synthetic wigs but last a little longer and look and feel even more natural like human hair wigs. The blend mixes high-grade heat-resistant synthetic fibers with real human hair which allows more flexibility than regular synthetics. They are not as pricey as full human hair wigs and range between $75 and $600, depending on the cap construction and the brand.

4. Human Hair Wigs is the superior choice for quality because they offer the most natural look and feel. They are the most versatile because they can be cut, styled, and sometimes colored to suit your desire. Most times it's hard to know exactly where the human hair came from. Sometimes it comes

from a donor or corpse but often human hair wigs are made from Asian hair. Other human hair may be Indonesian, Indian, European, and now Brazilian. Asian hair tends to be thicker and extremely straight which makes it harder to hold a curl. Indonesian hair is a little less costly and is often used for ethnic style wigs because of its texture. European hair has the highest demand, is very hard to get, and is very costly. Indian hair is similar to European hair because it is thinner but with more texture. Indian hair is the most popular for its wet and wavy look. Virgin Russian hair is very fine but very durable. It is the most sought after hair in the world and also the most expensive as 16 inches can cost up to $10,000.

THE HAIR COMMANDMENTS

Photos courtesy: Stylist Egypt Buck

In addition to the origin of the human hair, you also need to consider how it is processed. When higher grade chemicals are used to color and texture the hair, the hair is more expensive. These chemicals are used to sanitize the hair as well as color and texture treat it. Human hair requires a lot of maintenance and must be conditioned and hydrated often as they do not receive the nutrients from your scalp like human hair that grows from your own follicles. Human hair is expensive so be careful of imitations. Many brands say the hair is human when it really isn't. Knockoff companies use descriptive words like "looks like and human hair quality" which are NOT the same as actual human hair. Real human hair wigs can range from $300 to thousands of dollars. Also keep in mind that human hair wigs are rarely ready to wear and may take some professional styling.

I. **The Pros to human hair**
   - Natural look and feel
   - Last longer
   - Versatility with styles
   - Virgin unprocessed hair can be dyed

II. **The Cons to human hair**
   - More expensive
   - The styles do not stay and styling has to be done often.
   - More maintenance.
   - Susceptible to humidity.

- Some products that say "human hair" actually are not.

C. **Cap Construction - The cap of the wig is basically the core (base). It is used to attach the hair which makes it a wig.**

1. The cap is made of different materials which can determine the wigs durability, weight, and the way the hair flows. There are four general cap constructions that feature various benefits. Please understand that depending on the brand, cap constructions can be trademarked and may offer additional features or combinations of the following cap descriptions.

Cap Construction Descriptions
What features work for you

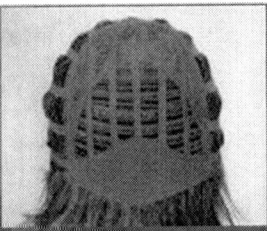

BASIC / TRADITIONAL
- The hair wefts are sewn into the shape of the cap.
- Durable and superior ventilation
- Volume is typically built in the crown
- Full coverage
- Adjustable tabs
- Ear tabs

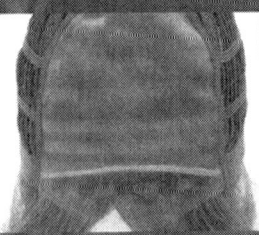

LACE FRONT
- Natural looking hair line
- Adhesive may be applied for more security
- Great for styling away from the face
- Transparent mesh of the lace creates a natural hairline by letting your skin show through

MONOFILAMENT
- Offers a combination of versatility & durability
- In the part looks like natural hair growth.
- A a sheer mesh made of strong synthetic fiber
- The hair strands are individually hand-tied to the monofilament segment of the cap.
- Double monofilament caps are goods for sensitive scalps and those with no hair as the cap is soft

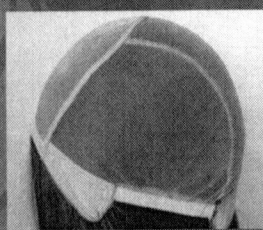

100% HAND-TIED
- The most natural look
- Allows superior versatility
- Every hair is individually tied by hand to a soft mesh cap
- Even up close it gives the most natural appearance of hair growth
- Generally the most expensive

With the help of advance technology wigs and the way that they are constructed have come along way. Choose the construction type that will be the most comfortable and fulfilling for you. There are great benefits to them all.

D. Wig Colors

Choosing the right hair color could be quite the challenge because many brands offer a wide variety of colors. The variety of options and the lack of commitment makes trying a new color exciting and fun. Different brands offer different colors depending on style and cap construction so we suggest finding your desired style and then selecting the color that will work best for you.

Matching Your Own Color
If you are looking to match your own natural color, choose a color that is a pinch lighter than your natural hair color. Most wigs are a blend of shades that provide the most authentic and natural look.

Trying Something New
Selecting a color that has high lights nor low lights blended with your natural shade is a great way to experiement with something new. It's not a drastic change but it will still be noticeable.

Most wig salons and beauty supply stores should carry swatches to help you find the perfect match. Keep in mind that wig brands trademark their own colors so a color in one specific brand may be different in another brand.

I. HOW LONG DOES A WIG LAST

The longevity of a wig depends on several things:
- **Your body chemistry and perspiration habits.**
  - Sweat and body heat can cause a wig to breakdown. This will shorten the life of your wig.

- If you sweat frequently and get hot easily it is recommended to wear a cool mesh cap under your wig. This will help absorb some of the perspiration before it reaches the cap construction of the wig and the wig hair.
- Also if you totally love a certain style buy two at the same time. The one could be used for everyday use (gym, shopping, work, and etc.). The other will be reserved for occasions and times when you want to look your best.

➢ **How well you take care of "her".**
- Wig maintenance is very important to the longevity of your wig. Whether human or synthetic, the hair is not growing from your scalp. Therefore, it does not receive the nutrition from your body or the nutrients it needs to stay vibrant. Just like a flower separated from its roots, proper nutrition is needed or it will look dry, brittle, limp, and will eventually appear lifeless.

➢ **The type of wig cap construction and the hair type.**
- Cap construction and hair type are major factors in longevity and varies by the need of the individual.

II. HOW DO YOU TAKE CARE OF THEM?

To maintain the maximum look and feel of your wig, synthetic hair and human hair both have special needs. Wigs and extensions go through intense chemical processing during production so upkeep is necessary to maintain natural movement and look. The type of products that you use is crucial along with the way you care for your unit.

It is not necessary to cleanse your wig daily. It is best to wait until it is actually dirty or has residue to completely wash your wig. Otherwise there are other steps you can take before or after each wear.

➢ **Washing: When & How**
- *When* - You should wash your wig when it becomes stiff, doesn't smell pleasant, or becomes sweaty. Unless you are experiencing one of these issues, the typical time span to wash your wig is about every 21 days.

- *What to use* – Be certain to use products that are made for your wig's hair type.
    o If your unit is synthetic, use shampoos/cleansers and conditioners that says "for synthetic wigs". There are many brands to choose from. Try ROP (Rene of Paris), Revlon, or Jacquelyn.

- o If your unit is human, you should use shampoos/cleansers and conditioners formulated for human hair wigs and hair pieces. Although the hair is human you do not want to use products that you would use on your own hair that grows from your scalp. The hair still needs proteins that the body produces naturally so using the proper shampoo will revitalize the wig. Also try to use cleansers that are **phosphate-free and sulfate-free** as this will help keep color treated hair vibrant.

- *How to wash* – Be certain your wig is free from any tangles prior to washing. Washing synthetic wigs is slightly different from washing human hair wigs.
  - o You will need to brush and comb your wig starting from the bottom and working your way to the top. This will help detangle any knots.
  - o FOR SYNTHETIC WIGS - fill a sink or basin with cool water and add shampoo. The amount of cleanser that you use depends on the thickness and length of your wig. For short and thinner wigs, use about a nickel size amount of cleanser. For longer and thicker wigs,

THE HAIR COMMANDMENTS

use about a quarter size amount. Adjust as needed depending on how dirty the wig is and again the thickness and length.
- Swish the wig around in the basin, using your hands to apply a little shampoo along the inside of the wig band. Do not do this to the entire cap. With the excess shampoo on your hand, distribute it from the roots to the tips of the wig.
- FOR HUMAN HAIR WIGS – You do not want to submerge the full cap into water as it will cause the hair to tangle and matte. Instead, first rinse the wig in cool to lukewarm water allowing the water to flow in the same direction as the hair. Next, take an appropriate amount of cleanser into your hand and work from the roots to the tips of the wig. Then use a little more shampoo to rub into the inside cap along the wig band.
- Next, for synthetic and human hair wigs, rinse the wig with cool water allowing the water to flow in the direction of the hair from root to tips to avoid tangling. Do not ring or twist the wig.

➢ **Conditioning – When & How**
- There are two types of conditioner: rinse out and leave-in revitalizer. The rinse out shampoo should be applied after washing your wig while

it is still wet. Leave-in spray conditioner is used as a revitalizer between washes and can be applied dry. However, leave-in conditioner may be applied after washing as well.

- RINSE OUT CONDITIONER - After washing the wig apply the conditioner into small sections of the wig massaging from the roots working down to the tips. Be careful to avoid the actual cap of the wig as it can cause the hair to loosen from the construction and create shedding. Once conditioner has been applied, let it set for about three minutes and then rinse it out with cool water while letting the water flow in the direction of the hair from root to tip.
- LEAVE-IN CONDITIONER – If your wig needs a little revitalizing between washes or if you do not have the time to do a complete condition after washing, a leave-in conditioner is a perfect solution. Again be certain that you are using products that are specifically made for your wig type. Almost all leave-in conditioners are sprays that you should use at least 10 inches away from the wig. Be certain to spray it evenly and avoid the actual cap.

➢ **Drying – proper drying methods are essential to the upkeep of the wig.**
- Be certain NEVER to ring or twist the hair and NEVER brush the hair while wet. Avoid drying on wig stands as it can cause

THE HAIR COMMANDMENTS

stretching or shrinking of the cap depending on the construction.
- Hair dryers should never be used on synthetic wigs as it can damage the fibers. Instead, air dry by placing it on a tall or hanging object such as a hair spray can, shower head, or laying it on a towel. It is okay to blot the wig with a towel prior to letting it air dry to help speed up the drying process.
- In some cases, hair dryers are okay to use on human hair wigs but be certain to keep the setting low and dry evenly.

➢ **Brushing – using the proper brush and brushing technique is essential to the look and longevity of a wig. Without proper brushing the wig will tangle, knot, lose luster, and look ratty.**
- *The proper brush* – It is best to use brushes that are designed for wigs. These brushes will have stiff bristles or teeth that are widely spaced apart. This will help detangle while keeping the fibers intact. The proper brush may have wire or plastic bristles/teeth. Also a paddle brush is appropriate.

-

- *How to brush* – Start brushing from the tips of the hair and work your way up to the root of the wig. Be gentle so the hair stays on the weft or cap. Keep in mind that rough and vigorous brushing can severely damage the wig. Be sure to brush over and on top of the hair.

III. HOW DO I PUT ON A WIG?

When putting on a wig, you should consider how you blend in your natural hair, whether you should wear a cap, and how to actually put it on.

- **Do you want to blend in your natural hair** – Depending on the cap construction, hair type, and color, blending some of your natural hair around the hairline and nape can make a wig look beyond belief natural.
    - In this case, section off your baby hair and about a half-inch of the hair around your hairline.
- **Should you wear a wig cap** – The use of a cap is personal preference. Some people find them uncomfortable, too tight, and at times they experience headaches from wearing a cap. Other people like the security the cap provides and that it keeps their hair protected and in place under the wig.
    - If you opt to wear a cap, be certain that it is placed just behind your hairline. DO NOT

wear it like a hat because you will see it at the base of your wig.
- There are other things that you can wear besides a wig cap such as a wig liner or wig band that serve the same purpose.

How do I actually put it on – Most wigs have ear tabs on each side that can be used as a guide.
- Hold the wig by the ear tabs with cap construction facing up and pull the wig onto your head.
- If the wig has long or full hair you may want to put it on from back to front to keep the hair in place. Shorter wigs can be put on from front to back.
- Once the wig is on, adjust it according to style and comfort. Check the back and sides to make sure everything is properly in place.
- If you left some of your natural hair out blend it in with the wig. Sometimes simple brushing works depending on hair texture. You can use a light pomade or gel to further blend and to mix texture.

IV. HOW DO I MAKE SURE IT IS SECURE SO IT WON'T SHIFT, SLIDE, OR FALL OFF?

Some wigs come with combs or they are just a perfect fit where you may not experience slippage. However, some people are prone to slippage and shifting because of their head shape or hair texture. In these cases, use bobby pins, no slip bands, or adhesives.

- Using bobby pins is an old school remedy that wig wearers have used for years. It is best to use this

remedy with basic cap construction wigs and without a wig cap. If you braid your natural hair you can pin the wig to your braids for a secure fit. If you choose to wear a wig cap, you will have to force the bobby pins through puncturing the cap.
- No slip bands are great for people with natural silky hair, people who sweat a lot, and for those who do not want to wear a cap. The benefits of these bands are:
    - They secure the wig in place without the use of glues or tapes.
    - They are not as stressful on your head and scalp, eliminating headaches.
    - The fabric is soft so it does not cause tension around your hairline. (Tension can lead to thinning).
- For an extra secure fit, use adhesives, double-sided wig tape or wig glue. It is best to use these adhesives with lace wigs, hand-tied wigs, and monofilament wigs, which all have a shear layer to apply the adhesive.
    - Double-sided wig tape should be applied to the hairline after prepping the hair line. First clean it with alcohol. Wig prep-specific products called skin protector and cleanser are great. But alcohol will suffice as well.
    - After prepping the hairline, measure where and how long you want to leave the tape by holding a strip up to the front side of your hairline and cutting the width and length of the tape accordingly. Repeat on the other

THE HAIR COMMANDMENTS

side with another piece of tape and then the mid front.
- After you have the tape cut to the size need peel the back off and put it in place starting with the sides first. Keep the front adhesive protecting paper on the opposite side of the tape and rub it to make certain it has a firm stick to your hairline.
- Next remove the side up adhesive protecting paper on all of the tape strips.
- Then put on your wig making sure the sides line up and the front is in its proper place. Rub the wig along the tape for a secure fit and let it set for a minute before styling.
  - The use of wig glues are a little more complicated as some people may have skin allergies. Do an allergy test prior to using the glue. Take a dab of glue and place it on a small part of your hairline (front or back wherever you feel most comfortable and able to take a close look). Leave it on for about an hour and then check your reaction. If you do not experience any breakouts or skin irritation, you should be okay. However, keep in mind long-term use of glues can cause serious damage which we will discuss further under the risks and dangers.

Prep your hairline using the same directions as if you were using tape.

- After prepping your hairline, try on your wig to check positioning. Using a light color eyeliner make a mark where the wig lining stops around your hairline. DO NOT draw a complete line. Just put a few subtle marks on both sides of the front and on the middle front.
- Take the wig off. Apply the glue right above the marks you made but applying across the entire hairline.
- Once the glue is applied, let it set for about 3-5 minutes (until it is tacky). Be very gentle and careful when making sure the hair lines match up. To avoid the hair sticking to the glue be certain to put the hair of the wig in a clip or bobby pin away from the face.
- Once your natural hairline is matched up with the wig hair line, firmly press it against the glue and let it completely dry before styling.

Please keep in mind applying a full lace or custom unit takes skill. Have a professional apply it for the first time.

THE HAIR COMMANDMENTS

Model: Cristal Joshua **Photo courtesy:** Stylist Egypt Buck

V. WILL EVERYONE KNOW I AM WEARING A WIG?

It depends on the wig. Some wigs definitely have a "wiggy" look while others look and feel natural. Wig wearing pros may be able to spot a wig on someone else but the average person may have no clue when someone is wearing a wig.
- For best results, shop in person (not online) for your wig. This allows you to try it on for style and fit.
- Follow the how to shop guide to help find the most natural looking wig for you.
- Celebrities have fooled us for years by wearing wigs. Some of the most famous wig-wearing celebrities include: Michael Jackson; Beyonce; Eva Gabor; Sherri Shepherd; and more.

VI. ARE WIGS HOT, HEAVY, AND IRRITATING?

Wigs can be hot, heavy, and irritating, depending on the individual. However, wigs have come a long way and with the different cap constructions and hair these annoyances can be combated. To make your wig-wearing experience as comfortable and successful as possible, try these steps.
- Choose a cap construction that is comfortable, making sure the size is accurate and the cap construction fits your needs.
- Find the best under wig method for you. If caps are irritating, try the other options that were provided.

- Check the weight of the wig. Lightweight wigs usually weigh 1 ounce to 2.5 ounces.
- Use proper hair and scalp treatments under your wig.
- Wear your wig as much as possible when you are by yourself so that you build self-confidence. The first time wearing a wig might feel strange. You may experience some insecurities but the more you wear it the more confident and accustomed to it you become.
- Shop according to the season. Some wigs come with the same style in different cap constructions. You can go with a breathable monofilament in the summer but a basic cap in the winter.

VII. ARE THERE ANY DANGER AND RISKS WHEN WEARING WIGS?

There are risks and danger that are associated with wearing wigs. Most are avoidable with proper use. Some risks include traction alopecia or hair loss, skin irritation and rashes, and headaches.

- Traction alopecia or hair loss can occur if the wig is too tight and worn too often. Some women who wore wigs for years without letting their hair breathe developed traction alopecia, which is caused when the dermal papilla and hair follicle are damaged from the constant pulling and rubbing of the hairline. To avoid traction alopecia:
    - Take breaks from wearing wigs to allow your scalp and follicles to breathe.

- Treat your hair and scalp properly as described in the under wig care section.
- Be certain not to braid or pull your natural hair too tight.
- If you notice thinning in certain areas where the wig rubs, stop wearing the wig and treat the area before it worsens.

  ❖ Skin irritations can occur from allergies to the fiber of the wig. If you experience these irritations:
  ❖ Try a different type of hair. You may need to choose a high grade synthetic or human hair. Consider seeing a dermatologist to locate the true source of the irritation and then be certain to avoid it.
  ❖ If the irritation only occurs in certain areas, for instance on the side of your face, consider choosing a style that is away from your face.
  ❖ Be certain to keep the wig clean.

o More serious infections can occur with the continued use of wig adhesives. It has been reported that ignoring skin infections can result in death. One of the most highly profiled issues with lace front wig glue is the story of Countess Vaughn, who wore lace wigs nonstop for years. She had an allergy to the glue but ignored many early warning signs. Eventually it got worse and caused skin discoloration around her hairline, ears, and under

THE HAIR COMMANDMENTS

her eyes. Some of her symptoms included oozing around her hairline, nape, and ears. She explained that the puss had a horrible smell and was very painful. To avoid this from happening:

- Do an allergy test with adhesive prior to using.
- Keep the applied site clean and let it breathe often.
- Do not use the glue for excessive amounts of time. We recommend two weeks on two days off for no longer than a two-month period before letting your hair completely breathe for at least a week.
- Checkout actress Countess Vaughn's story about her lace wig adhesive experience. http://www.thedoctorstv.com/videolib/init/11166

o Wigs may cause headaches due to the added pressure on your head.

- Proper fit and cap construction is very important in avoiding headaches. Make sure that your wig is not too tight as well as any caps or liners that you may wear.
- Keep the wig clean as well proper hair care for your natural hair and scalp.

VIII. HOW DO I TAKE CARE OF MY HAIR AND SCALP UNDER THE WIG?

Under wig care is the most important element of wearing a wig. Without proper under wig care you can experience hair loss, scalp, damage, headaches, dandruff, and more.

    A. Taking care of your scalp under your wig
- i. Be certain to let your scalp breathe by taking breaks from wearing wigs.
- ii. Keep your scalp moisturized with natural oils and massaging. (coconut oil, grape seed oils, and shea butters are great natural products to use on your scalp).
- iii. Keep the scalp clean and conditioned.
- iv. Make sure to maintain a healthy diet and exercise regimen. Drinking lots of water is essential to your skin and scalp.

    B. Taking care of your natural hair under your wig
- i. Comb your hair daily if the wig is glued or taped down.
- ii. Keep your hair clean and conditioned.
- iii. Deep condition your hair at least once a month.

THE HAIR COMMANDMENTS

iv. Cut split ends and trim your hair when needed.
v. DO NOT pull your hair tightly.
vi. Be certain to follow the instructions in the natural hair section if you are trying to grow your natural hair under your wig.

Model: Asia Mason-Martin **Photographer:** Mr. Don Photos

THE SHALLS FOR WIGS

1. Thou shall know that every wig is not for everyone.
2. Thou shall make sure to wear the proper size and adjustments.
3. Thou shall brush the wig thoroughly starting from the bottom to the top.
4. Thou shall use the proper products depending on the hair type of the wig.
5. Thou shall know when it is time to purchase another wig.
6. Thou shall take care of the scalp and hair even when wearing wigs.
7. Thou shall keep the wig clean to avoid irritation.
8. Thou shall be aware of what you are purchasing and remember that everything that says human hair may not really be human hair.
9. Thou shall be careful when using wig adhesives and bonds.
10. Thou shall wear your wig with confidence, comfort, and grace.

THE SHALL NOTS FOR WIGS

1. Thou shall not choose a wig because it looked good on someone else.
2. Thou shall not use the same products on a wig that you would use for natural hair.
3. Thou shall not brush the hair from the root as it will cause shedding.
4. Thou shall not brush or comb the wig while it is wet after washing.
5. Thou shall not dry the wig on a head as it can change the construction size by shrinking it smaller than your head size or expanding it larger than your head size.
6. Thou shall not neglect your natural hair and scalp when wearing a wig.
7. Thou shall not neglect the care of a wig and let it get old and brittle.
8. Thou shall not chose styles and colors that are not flattering to your face shape or skin tone.
9. Thou shall not judge others who wear wigs.
10. Thou shall not wear a wig that makes you uncomfortable.

WEAVES

Many people wear weaves to enhance the hair that they already have, to protect their own hair, and because many times it is easier to achieve and maintain styles with weave. When we mention weave, we basically are referring to hair that comes on a weft aka track hair. This type of hair can be applied many ways as discussed throughout this chapter. Knowing what weave will work best for you may depend on texture, length, and price. When shopping for weaves, many believe the most expensive choice is usually the best but that just is not true. Most hair weave is made from donors but can come from other sources such as a corpse and manufactured cloned human hair. Here are answers to the most frequently asked weave questions and perceptions.

What are the different qualities?
Hair weave comes in synthetic, heat friendly synthetic, human hair blend, and several types of human hair.

> A) **Synthetic Weaves** are made of a blend of synthetic fibers such as acrylic. This type of weave cannot take any heat. It is the least expensive and may cause allergic reactions to those with sensitive skin. It is good to use as a filler in a bun or ponytail, styles that you do not need to last a long time, and if price is an issue. Synthetics have come a long way as some brands make synthetic weaves that actually feel and look like real human hair. There are also synthetic weaves that come pre-curled which makes it easier to achieve more styles for less.

- Synthetic weaves do not take heat
- May tangle quickly
- May cause allergic reactions
- Should not be worn for long periods of time as they do not hold their quality
- Are inexpensive (you can expect to pay $13 to $30 for enough hair to complete a full style)
- Should not be reused
- Could last up to a week or longer depending on maintenance and activity

B) **Heat-Friendly Synthetics** are made with higher grades of synthetic fibers. This type of hair can take low heat with a special technique. After applying low heat, hold the hair in your hand until the curl completely cools then release it. This grade is better than basic synthetic hair but not as good a quality as human hair blends or human hair. Some styles come pre-curled making the style last longer. This type of hair is used more to do quick weaves and may last up to two weeks.
- Takes a low setting on a heating tool (curling iron, flat iron, etc.)
- May tangle
- May cause allergic reactions
- Cost a little more than synthetic hair (priced between $15-$45 depending on length and brand. Estimate is based on 16-inch length)
- Should not be reused

WIGS, WEAVES, AND NATURAL HAIR

Model: Dawn Angela Mickens   **Photographer:** JWJ Photography

C) **Trademarked Fibers of Synthetics include:**
   - Kanekalon Fibers – composed of two monomers acrylonitrile and vinyl chloride. The hair feels natural and soft with natural body movement.
   - Futra Fiber – this synthetic fiber is heat friendly
   - Ultima Fiber – is manmade from natural collagen protein that gives the hair a moist and rich natural shine. This type of synthetic has many characteristics of human hair.
   - Keralon – is also heat friendly synthetic.

D) **Human Hair Blends** are made with higher grades of synthetic fibers and blended with human hair. It blends the best of both fibers. Depending on the brand and quality, the human hair percentage can range from 10 percent to 80 percent. The higher the percentage of human hair, the better the quality of the weave. Some brands that claim to be human hair are actually human hair blends. You can usually apply light heat to the hair and it feels more like human hair than synthetics but they will not last as long as human hair in most cases. Human hair blends can come straight, textured, or pre curled. Depending on maintenance and human hair percentage, human hair blends can last for months. Overall human hair blends offer the

ease of synthetic but looks like human hair and is easy to change the styles.
- Holds a style like high grade synthetics.
- Looks and feels like human hair
- Doesn't cost as much as human hair but more expensive than synthetics (ranges in price from $25 to $65, depending on length and brand. Estimate is based on 16-inch length)
- Does not last as long as properly cared for human hair
- May be reused but not likely as it may not keep its luster
- The color is stable and remains close to original state.

E) **Human Hair** has the most natural look and feel. In most cases, it is soft and has natural movement. Choosing human hair is the most complicated because of the varieties and authenticity. The most popular characteristics to consider are texture, longevity, process, and price. The texture determines the price and how long the weave will last with proper maintenance. When purchasing human hair, read the labels carefully and look for descriptive words such as feel, look, quality, and like. These words usually indicate the hair is NOT human but a clone of some sort.

THE HAIR COMMANDMENTS

Model: Aquarius Williams

1. The most popular and attainable textures of human hair weave include silky straight, yaki, Malaysian, Indian, Brazilian, and other exotic textures.

   a. **Silky Straight Weave** – has probably been around longer than any other weave texture. It is typically made from Asian hair, more specifically Chinese hair. The hair is extremely straight and can be difficult to hold a curl or style. This hair should be used for straight styles or styles that will be pinned. There was a time when silky straight hair was the most popular and easy to find hair in beauty supply stores. However, with the influx of different human hair textures, silky straight is not as popular and harder to find now.

b. **Yaki Weave** – has more texture to it and the term is used to describe weave that resembles different types of African-American hair. Most yaki hair comes from Indonesians or Asians but is treated to give it texture. The process of yaki can be applied to any type of hair from synthetics to Remy. Yaki hair may come in four textures – silky, which resembles relaxed African-American hair; regular yaki that looks more like relaxed hair that is not silky and shiny; kinky yaki that resembles African-American hair that has not been chemically treated; and coarse yaki that looks like untreated Afro Caribbean hair, which may be curly or wavy.

c. **Malaysian Hair Weave** – is one of the highest grades of weave on the market. It is typically dark in color, with a smooth sheen, and natural moisture. The fine texture can be bleached, colored, and cut to desired style. The hair is extremely soft and has a wave to it that can be straightened, curled, or left natural. It does not curl or wave additionally when wet. This hair is pretty rare and more expensive than "regular" human hair. When discussing Malaysian hair, it can be used to describe the actual Malaysian hair as well as a weaving technique. When shopping for hair, make sure the sales rep knows the difference and shows you the correct products.

d. **Indian Hair Weave** – is straight like European hair but thicker and has more texture. The denier (unit of fineness) is thin and the hair is rounded. The hair is more resistant to breakage and shedding. Indian hair follicles are straight which makes the hair straight sort of like European hair but its thickness and more coarse texture allows the hair to hold a curl or wave. Indian weave is highly sought because of the process of Remy that most Indian hair is accompanied by. The Remy process is fully explained later. Indian hair can be costly depending on the Remy process and brand. Many believe the price is worth it because of its longevity. The hair has a natural sheen and the strands are thick and healthy. Some Indian hair may wave or curl when wet, giving it more versatility, style and natural charm.

e. **Brazilian** – is one of the most recent popular textures of hair weave. This hair can come in different grades ranging from 1 (poorest) to 5A (the best). The grades are based on the process, origin, and donor of the hair. It is coarser than Indian hair. It holds a curl better than most textures of hair and has a natural original shine. Brazilian hair should be able to dye depending on how it has been processed and treated. Due to its coarseness, it may tangle and become dry. Therefore, conditioning and proper care is key to maintenance and longevity. This hair is harder to achieve bone straight styles but blends better with the natural hair of people of color. The popularity of Brazilian hair raises the risks of the hair not being authentic so carefully read labels and be skeptical of low prices. The price will vary based on brand and location. Typically Brazilian hair is much more expensive than "regular" weave, comparable to Indian hair weave, but less expensive than European hair.

   f. **Peruvian Hair Weave** – is the coarsest of the textures mentioned and holds curls very well. Its thickness makes it great for styles that require volume and blending the hair works better for people of color. This hair is rare and more expensive than Indian and Brazilian hair. It is not recommended for bone straight styles. Depending on how the hair is processed, it can be dyed and cut to the desired style. The vast majority of Peruvian hair comes from donors.

2. Human Hair Processing Methods effect the strength and quality of the hair. It also determines the price, longevity, look, and feel of the hair.
   a. *Processed hair* is dyed and processed for cleanliness using harsh chemicals. This makes the hair look less natural, hard or impossible to self-dye, and it may not last as long. Chemicals are needed to sanitize and strip away the natural color and texture so that different texture patterns and color can be added to

the hair. This hair usually comes in recognizable colors like 1b, 1, 2, 4 and so on. This processing uses low quality chemicals that are very harsh and effect the integrity of the hair.

b. *Virgin Hair* refers to hair that went through processing with higher quality chemicals or a more organic processing approach. It produces higher quality, more expensive. It has not been artificially curled or straightened and should be free of dyeing and bleaching. The benefits of its natural state allows you to custom dye it to match your hair. This option is also best for those with allergies and skin irritations. The hair feels and moves more naturally and should last longer.

3. The technique used to collect the hair from donors impacts the quality, look, and feel of the weave as well. Hair that is collected from several donors and not cut from the cuticle results in a lower quality hair weave. The premium technique is a method called "Remy," where the hair follicles run in the same direction and the cuticle remains intact. This results in less tangling and a smoother feel. The Remy method can then be processed or left unprocessed. Therefore,

a premium selection of hair weave could be Virgin Indian Remy which means the Indian hair has the cuticle intact running in one direction and has not been processed using harsh chemicals.

How do I determine which lengths to buy and how much will I need?

Determining length and how much to purchase are based on personal preference. The first thing to consider is the style that you want to achieve. Next, you will need to measure and estimate.

- **Style/Application** – after choosing a style, you will need to figure out the weaving method that you will use, such as full sew-in, partial sew-in, glued full quick weave, or just adding a few tracks to your natural hair. These methods are discussed in detail in the next section.
- **Measuring and estimating** – once the style and the method of application is chosen, measure the length that you want the hair. The most effective way to measure is to use a measuring tape on the inches side. Starting at one inch (do not start at 0 as the extra inch will allow space for cutting and shaping in the end). At the top of the nape, measure down to the longest point that you want the hair to stop and write the amount of inches. If the style you are trying to achieve is all one length without any layers this length will be the shortest length needed. If the style you desire has layers and the bottom layer is

the longest, this is longest length that you will need. Next, use the same method and start at the top of your head down to the desired length. For an all one length style you would stop at the same point as the nape measurement and this will be the longest length weave need. If the desired style is layered, stop where the shortest layer will be, this will be the shortest length of weave need. To make things less complicated, some people purchase all one length of hair (the longest) and then cut to style. Although it may seem easier, it can result in waste of hair and money.

What options do I have for hair weave application? There are many different techniques for attaching weave with today's technology. The most popular applications are: full sew-ins; partial sew-ins; quick weave gluing; partial glue-ins; clip-ins; and hot/cold fusions.

1. Full sew-ins require all of the natural hair to be braided. The way the hair is braided depends on the stylists' technique. To protect the hair and to provide a smoother natural look, some stylists prefer to sew a weaving cap onto the braids. This can decrease breakage to the natural hair and may also hold the style longer. Next, using a hair weaving needle and thread, the weave is sewn onto the cap or braided natural hair. The biggest benefit of a sew-in is the protection it provides your natural hair. For best results, be certain the braids and sew-in do not pull on the

natural hair too tightly. Also be certain the scalp can still be moisturized when needed. This method is one of the most expensive because the time and skill that it requires to apply.

2. Partial sew-ins are used to describe the hair only being partially braided and some of the natural hair is left out to blend in with the hair weave. Depending on the desired style, the stylist may leave a small portion, sections or a large portions of the natural hair out. The magic in this style is in the blending. This requires the selection of hair weave that is close to your natural hair texture. The risk is heat damage if heat is needed to style the natural hair or to blend the natural hair to the hair weave. The benefit of a partial sew-in is how natural it looks, feels, and moves. The price for a partial sew-in is moderate depending on stylists and style.

3. Quick hair glue-ins require the natural hair to be molded using setting lotions, gel, spritz, or other hair molding products. Usually, you will be placed under a dryer until the hair becomes hard and completely dry. Some stylists use hair protectors such as Morning Glory or wrapping papers, which are applied on top of the mold to ensure firmness and that all of the natural hair is protected. The weave is then glued onto the mold in the desired style. This method is

quicker than a sew in and does not cost as much. However, the style does not last as long as a sew-in and it may cause skin irritation. When taking the quick weave out, use caution not to rip it off the mold as it can damage your natural hair.

THE SHALLS FOR WEAVES

1. Thou shall choose the weave that will work best with your texture, style, and budget.
2. Thou shall select weave that will not cause skin irritation.
3. Thou shall brush weave thoroughly starting from the bottom to the top to decrease shedding.
4. Thou shall use the proper products on the weave for maintenance, cleaning, and shine.
5. Thou shall choose the best method of weave application for your hair and budget.
6. Thou shall take care of the scalp and hair even when wearing weaves.
7. Thou shall know when it is time to take the weave out.
8. Thou shall be aware of what you are purchasing and remember that everything that says human hair might not really be human hair.
9. Thou shall maintain moisture at all times.
10. Thou shall be confident and comfortable with your weave.

THE SHALL NOTS FOR WEAVES

1. Thou shall not neglect your natural hair and scalp when wearing a weave.
2. Thou shall not braid the hair tight when wearing sew-ins.
3. Thou shall not let the weave develop build up and bacteria.
4. Thou shall not wash the weave without brushing and untangling it first.
5. Thou shall not use adhesives and removal methods that will pull out your natural hair.
6. Thou shall not wear weaves for an extensive amount of time without letting your scalp breathe.
7. Thou shall not neglect the care of a weave by letting it mat or tangle.
8. Thou shall not leave a painful weave in.
9. Thou shall not judge others who wear weaves.
10. Thou shall not use a micro-fiber towel to dry your weave.

NATURAL HAIR

Having natural hair is something that many women proudly embrace. Some women have always had natural hair but others may have made a switch from relaxed hair, heat treated hair, or extensions and weaves. When deciding to go from treated hair to natural hair, there are many things that women should consider, including: will you do a big chop or transition by letting the treated hair grow out; what texture type is your hair; what remedies will work best for your hair maintenance and growth; what type of products you should use; how much time will you need to spend on your hair; and what styles will you wear. Most importantly remember everyone's hair journey is unique. What worked and looked right to one may not be the same case for someone else. It will take time and research for some women to be comfortable with their natural hair where others may totally love and embrace it from the beginning.

The Big Chop

When deciding to transition from treated hair to natural hair, you must first decide what length you would like to begin your journey. Some women take the plunge and go bald or very short. This is called the big chop. Cutting out all of the treated hair is liberating for some. It allows you to start the journey faster and the short or bald style can be very easy to maintain. The wash and go routine that many women experience after the big chop frees up time and provides a carefree journey. There are less cares about the weather or having a bad hair day. Another benefit of the "big chop" is that all of your hair will basically be one texture, which is easier because you will use the same routine and the same products for all of your hair. Think of the money and time you can save.

Some of the disadvantages with the big chop could include not liking your short style, not knowing how to care for the style at first, fewer style options, and the response you may get from others. When taking the big chop, there is the possibility that you may not like the way you look with short hair. Some women do not like their head shape or head size with short hair. The truth is you might expect it to look a certain way but you might not. Initially, you will not have many style options until your hair grows out some. You might not receive positive and encouraging feedback after the big chop. Some people can be critical about your new short, natural style. This can be due to the resentment of change, conditioned thinking of beauty, or they genuinely do not care for the style on you.

Your hair and scalp may need time to adjust to the new routine and the lack of chemicals it was used to. This transition can take up to two years for some. As a result, you'll learn that certain remedies and products that used to work will no longer work. Your natural hair may take on many textures and patterns before settling into consistency.

Model: Keinu Sullivan **Photographer:** Jeff Martin

The best way to combat the disadvantages of the big chop is to be certain and confident it is for you. Here are some tips to help you along that journey:

1. Research prior to making the decision.
2. Pick some styles you may like from Pinterest, magazines, books, blogs, the internet, etc.
3. Buy some cool hair accessories, earrings, and make up (if you like these types of things) as they may help you embrace the look and style.
4. Build a great support system, join blogs, and talk to your family and friends about your decision.
5. Find a reputable natural hair stylist who will do your big chop and help you maintain your natural hair.
6. Celebrate the big chop with perhaps a party, event, or dinner.
7. Do it on your terms and do not compare yourself to others.
8. Weigh your options.

Transitioning

If you decide that the big chop just is not for you, consider letting your treated hair grow out to a length that you are more comfortable and confident with. This will give you the option to gradually become natural while still holding on to a piece of your comfort zone. To achieve this properly, it will take maintenance, care, time, and maybe more money on products. Working with two textures of hair can be costly and time consuming so be certain that's the route you wish to take. Achieving certain styles may be more of a challenge and it will be a longer conversion process. Some people experience a thick line of demarcation, the line where your treated hair and your natural hair meet. The hair at this line may be very fragile and prone to breakage. Many women notice when working with multiple textures they are mask one and define the other. Once the natural hair grows to a certain point you should consider doing a chop to cut away the remaining treated hair. This will tame some of the cumbersomeness of working with multiple textures.

Texture Types

Hair typing is a code that is used as a general guide to determine what type of texture the hair is. This will help find styles that will work best with your texture as well as products. There are different types of trademarked hair typing systems but most of them are based on the same five principles: curl/wave pattern; sponginess/ porosity; density; width; and length. Being that curl patterns, coils, and wave patterns are not the same, all of those things are taken into consideration when determining your hair type. After researching, interviewing, and experimenting we took a collective approach to describing hair typing.

Curl and Wave Patterns

One of the most common curl pattern systems is the Andre Walker Curl Typing System. In this approach hair curl patterns are broken down into four basic classifications; Type 1 Straight, Type 2 Wavy, Type 3 Curly, and Type 4 Kinky. Other systems break this down into more specific groups of each hair type.

- **Type 1 Straight** – is known as the most resilient type of hair because the straightness allows the natural oils to penetrate throughout the entire shaft of the hair strands. Straight hair usually has natural sheen and takes less maintenance and care to grow. There are different types of straight hair.
- **Type 1A** is straight fine hair which tends to be thin, soft, shiny but oily and hard to hold

curls and various hair styles. It also has to be washed often because of the build-up of oils it can collect. This hair type is common for Caucasian women.
- **Type 1B** is straight medium hair that typically has volume. It receives lots of natural oils but not as much as Type 1A and does not suffer from as much build up.
- **Type 1C** is straight thick or coarse hair. The hair is typically bone straight and may be harder to curl. This type of hair is most common for Asian women.

- **Type 2 Wavy** – has a definite 'S' pattern and falls in between straight and curly. This hair type is typically coarse and lays in a 'S' pattern against the scalp, unlike curly hair that stands away from the scalp. There are three subcategories to Type 2 Wavy hair:
- **Type 2A** is fine and generally easy to handle. Various styles can be achieved with this type of hair. It can be blown out without hassle for a straight look or made curly relatively easy. It also usually has natural sheen and should not be weighed down with heavy products. Use light weight products such as mousses and light gels to define waves. To achieve the most body, opt for sulfate-free cleansers, silicone free conditioners, and volumizer to decrease frizz.

- **Type 2B** is medium wavy and tends to stick to the scalp even if it is layered. This hair type tends to frizz and be more resistant to styling. Use light products to reduce frizz and to avoid build up.
- **Type 2C** is thicker with more waves. This type of hair is also resistant to certain styles and may frizz. The wave has more curl to it and requires more maintenance. Some type 2C textures may have a straight under layer or an even more curly under layer giving it a more ringlet look. Creamy products and heavier gels usually work better with Type 2C. When using a heavier amount of product, be certain to scrunch it into the hair which might be easier to achieve when using a microfiber towel.

- **Type 3 Curly** – this hair type has a definite curl pattern that is most prominent when it is dry or humid. As it absorbs water it tends to get curlier and sometimes more frizzy. It is also easy to style and has natural body. It can be straightened easily by blow drying. When Type 3 hair is healthy, it's shiny, soft, and full of strong elasticity. The hair can be stretched without breakage and might appear coarse but is actually soft and manageable.
  - **Type 3A** has defined 'S' pattern loose curls that are springy and bouncy. The loose curls can be a combination of textures and the

longer the hair, the more curl it will have. The climate highly effects Type 3A as humidity will cause it to frizz. The hair can be easily straightened with blow drying or heat. Sulfate-free cleansers will give the curls definition followed by a leave-in conditioner to hydrate and moisturize. Also the use of light gels and creams will help define the curls.

- **Type 3B** has springy and spirally curls that vary from ringlets to tight corkscrew-like curls. It can be big as it springs away from the scalp in abundance with the curliest part around the crown. The hair isn't shiny and can be pretty coarse. Straightening the hair will take work and time. The use of heavier gels and creams will help reduce frizz and define curls.

- **Type 3C** has voluminous tight corkscrew curls that are densely close together in straw-like circumference. The hair may be kinky and abundant causing it to be considered as big hair. Blow drying this hair straight is the most challenging out of three types of curly hair but it can be achieved with products that provide moisture and protection from heat. It is best to use moisturizing cleansers, nourishing conditioners, and hair milks, oils, and butters.

- **Type 4 Kinky** – Ranges from wiry and fine to coarse and thick. Typically the hair is tightly coiled which makes this hair type the most fragile. There are fewer cuticle layers which decreases the amount of protection from brushing and heat. Many strands are packed densely close together but the hair may still be fine. It does not have a shine but still possesses sheen and may vary from soft to rough to touch. The hair has elasticity that can be stretched for length.
- **Type 4A** is soft tightly coiled hair with a defined 'S' pattern. It has more moisture than other types of 4 but is still quite fragile. The hair lacks cuticle layers so it is very sensitive to combing and heat. It is easy to split and break so moisturizing it is the most important thing to growth and avoiding loss. Try a regimen that includes co-washing, condition, and moisturizing, which will keep the hair clean without stripping it of its natural oils. This should be done once a week to keep hair healthy and looking its best.
- **Type 4B** is wiry and coiled with less of a curl. The hair is more of a 'Z' pattern and bends in sharp angles. It is also very fragile and should be handled with care to avoid breakage. The hair feels like cotton and is tightly coiled with strands packed very closely. The hair lacks layers of cuticle and

needs protection from damage inflected by combing, brushing, heat, and even weather. It can shrink up to 75 percent, making it appear shorter than it actually is. For healthy hair use heavier hair products for co-washing, conditioning, and styling. Products such as puddings and creams tend to work best and remember to condition and moisturize about every three days.

The highest concern is keeping Type 4 hair healthy and growing because it is so fragile. Many experts refer to the Three M's which are Minimizing breakage, Maximizing growth, and Maintenance. To minimize breakage it is important to keep the hair moisturized and clean. This allows the natural oils to flourish and provide additional support to prevent the hair from becoming brittle. To maximize hair growth, it important to remember it's not only what you put on the hair but also what goes on with the body. Proper diet, exercise, and vitamins contributes to hair growth. If you are experiencing little to no hair growth it is best to see your physician and a dermatologist because there may be a deficiency or medical problem. Maintenance and consistency keeps the hair healthy and growing. Finding a regimen may be a little difficult because what works this week may not work the next week, especially in the beginning stages of going natural. It may take some experimenting with products but be consistent and allow your hair time to get use to the process.

Co-Washing

Co-washing is the application of using conditioners to cleanse your hair instead of shampoos. This a method that may work great for Type 4 textures of hair as it will not strip the hair of its natural oils. Many conditioners are formulated with ingredients that actually cleanse as well as condition and moisturize. Due to the silicones that provide shine from conditioners, co-washing will cause build up. The solution is to use conditioners that contain water-soluble silicones as they are easier to rinse thoroughly. Check the label for Dimethicone Copolyl and PEG Modified Dimethicone as these are the best types of conditioners for co-washing. Some naturals co-wash daily but some stick to their normal regimen at about once a week. The overall purpose of co-washing is to keep hair clean, moisturized, and healthy. We are not necessarily endorsing any particular product but many naturals and natural stylists like Carols Daughter Hair Milk Cleansing Conditioner. It is sulfate-free, color safe, and it does not lather up. It quickly detangles coils and kinks and allows you to finger through the hair. You do not have to opt for brands or expensive shampoos. Try different ones to see what works best for you.

Stretching

After washing, natural hair can shrink up to 75 percent making it appear shorter and tighter. This is a great asset for certain styles and looks. However, shrinkage may also cause tangling and breakage. To avoid the mishaps and achieve different styles, the hair may require some stretching, which is a term used to describe the process elongating the hair to reduce tangles and achieve length. There are different methods of stretching based on personal preference and skill. Most think it is easier to stretch when the hair is wet or damp, preferably after washing, co-washing, or conditioning. The four most popular ways to stretch hair are: banding; twisting; blow outs; and Bantu knots.

Banding

Banding is an easy and quick method to stretching the hair. Most people do not wear banding as an actual style but more as a method to achieve other styles. In this process, you will part your hair in several sections then use cloth covered bands or ponytail holders to wrap around each section. Start from the root and band all the way to the end of the hair leaving only about an inch uncovered. Longer hair will require several bands. Allowing the hair to dry while banded will stretch the hair but it may leave small indentions as well. Be certain to use strong fully clothed bands that do not have the metal clip as the metal connector will snag the hair and cause breakage.

Twisting

Twisting is a functional way to stretch as the twist can be worn as a style while waiting for the hair to dry and stretch. This method is simple and easy to put in and take out. Take two parts of the hair and wrap them around each other in a twisting motion all the way to the end. Some hair types may stay simply by twirling the twist at the end but other types may need a band at the end of the twist. The amount of twists will depend on the thickness of your hair. The twist will be springy so for more of a stretch, pin the twist around your head. When the twists are dry you can unravel them and wear your hair as is. The hair will be a little wavy and natural.

Blow Outs

Blow Outs are controversial with some naturals because of the use of heat. The setting does not have to be high on the blow dryer and you do not have to fully dry the hair. Heat is generally okay in moderation. You can part the hair in a few sections and as you blow dry each section, pull the hair in a stretching motion. Some people like using the blow dryer because it speeds up the process. If your hair type is a 4, be mindful of the heat setting to avoid any damage, excessive drying, and breakage.

Bantu Knots

Bantu Knots are easy and also functional. If you plan on wearing the Bantu knots as a style it will be best to actually part the hair and wind each section in one direction. Next, take the section and wrap it around to form a knot. To secure the knot tuck the ends underneath the knot. You may need to use a hair pin or bobby pin for extra security. The use of Bantu knots do not provide maximize stretching but it will stretch it some and provide a great style during and after unraveling the knot.

Natural Hair Styles

Deciding what type of natural styles you would like to wear will help determine what remedies and products will work best with your hair. Maintenance and consistency is important when working with natural styles so many women choose styles based on comfort and time. Natural styling can be broken into five categories: free of chemical treatment but heat and blow outs; afros; twists and braids; naturally curly; and bald.

Free of chemical treatment but heat and blow outs

There is a misconception that using heat on natural hair makes the hair "not natural". The truth is using heat in moderation and with protection can make the hair more manageable without damage. Many naturals who opt for heat like the versatility they can achieve with the length that blow drying and adding some heat provide. It is important to know your hair type and texture to understand what your hair can take and what products to use to protect it. If your hair is damaged, refrain from heat as much as possible because your cuticle layers may be stripped. In this case, the strands will not hold moisture and the heat will further damage the hair. Try these tips to successfully use heat on your natural hair:

- ✓ Use a ionic blow dryer.
- ✓ If blow drying once a week, use a cooler setting.
- ✓ If blow drying once a month, use a warmer/hot setting.
- ✓ Be certain that your hair is detangled prior to blow drying.
- ✓ Hold the dryer between 5-10 inches away from your head.

THE HAIR COMMANDMENTS

- ✓ Use the proper settings on flat irons and styling tools. Never go above 400 degrees.
- ✓ Use styling tools that are ceramic.
- ✓ Be certain the hair is moisturized and use heat protectants that work with your hair type.

Model: Lai-Ling Bernstein   **Photographer:** Dwayne Boyd

Afros

Afros are legendary and have been the representation of natural hair and black pride for centuries. All afros are unique based on their girth, texture, color, and the person who is rocking it. When going for the "big chop" many women opt for a "Teeny Weeny Afro" known by naturals as the TWA. Some people fall in love with their TWA so they keep it small but some let it grow out and rock a huge afro similar to that of legendary activist Angela Davis. Whatever your preference, it is important to keep the hair and scalp clean and healthy for the best results.

L. Denise Edwards

There are five basic steps to maintain a healthy afro: cleansing, moisturizing, trimming, picking, and plaiting. Following a cleansing regimen based on your hair texture type will keep your scalp clean and promote growth. Keeping the hair and scalp moisturized will prevent breakage and give your afro sheen and luster. Be careful not to oversaturate the scalp and do not use products that are too heavy for your hair type as this will weigh your afro down. Trimming your afro and making sure there aren't any split ends will keep it growing healthy and even. Many find picking and combing techniques that work best for their hair. Some choose to dampen the hair into sections, add a cream, and then pick out the hair closing the gaps from the parts. Plaiting your hair at night will help keep the moisture. Be certain to wear a satin hair cap or sleep on a satin pillow.

Model: Amy Lyn Elliott
Photography by: Aurora V Photography

WIGS, WEAVES, AND NATURAL HAIR

Model: Keinu Sullivan **Photographer:** Chuck Brown Photography

Twists and braids

Twists and braided styles are multi-functional as they can stretch and grow the hair while nicely styled and beautiful. Many naturals opt for these styles because of the easy maintenance and the protection they provide the hair if done properly. When deciding to wear these styles try doing some preventative work first to keep your natural hair healthy. Deep conditioning your hair with a strong protein formula prior to getting the twists and braids will help prepare your hair for the extra weight it is going to have. Be careful not to pull the hair too tightly to prevent breakage or even balding. Make sure if you are adding hair you do not make the braid larger than the part. Do not include all of your edges are baby hair because the hair is fine and fragile. If you must add hair around the edges keep it very light and again avoid pulling. Keep the scalp moisturized when wearing twist and braided styles.

Properly taking out braids and twists is just as important as how they are put in. The goal is to get all of the hair unraveled, moisturized, untangled, and cleaned with minimal new growth lost in the process. If it is hard to unravel the braids, use a mixture consisting of water, conditioner, and oil to make it easier, less brittle, and less fragile.

Model: Jeannine Oliver **Photographer:** Dwayne Boyd

Naturally curly

People with naturally curly hair know it's an adventure every day because the hair seems to have a mind of its own. When it feels like looking good it does. When it chooses to be combative, well, it shows. But more and more people are finding styles for their curly locks that accentuate their face and showcase natural beauty.

We suggest you experiment with different products and looks but knowing what your hair needs will help make the process better. When working with your natural hair eliminate heat altogether. Blow drying and using heat tools will change the curl pattern. If you are in a hurry and have to blow dry, use a diffuser. Remember that all curly hair is not the same. Finer hair might be easier to maintain and thicker hair might have more bounce. Consider these:

1. Do not shampoo your hair every day. However, co-washing or conditioning is good.
2. When washing or conditioning, do it in the shower or salon sink. This allows the curls to point downward and use cold water whenever rinsing your hair.
3. Avoid heavy oils. Try mousses, creams, and gel.
4. Do not towel dry your hair; Let it air dry.
5. Add products in your hair when wet for volume and body.
6. Be certain to detangle you hair before and after each wash.
7. Do not brush your hair when it is dry because it will cause frizz.
8. Keep ends trimmed and keep the hair shaped by cutting.

WIGS, WEAVES, AND NATURAL HAIR

Model: Alicia Redmond **Photographer:** Manual Craig

Model: Akia Uwanda   **Photographer:** HiDef Pixels

Bald

Short haircuts and the bald look are becoming more and more fashionable every day, even for some women forced to shave their heads because of disease or some other hair loss condition.

Women are owning the look and empowering themselves with their beauty. Everything from parts to waves to edges add personal effect to short and bald hair. The Bald Movement is a great example of that.

Model: Nell Coleman, founder The Bald Movement

Model: DeShelle Taylor
Photographer: M. Scott Whitson

THE SHALLS FOR NATURAL

1. Thou shall be patient when starting the process of going natural.
2. Thou shall use sulfate-free shampoos. Sulfates dry out your hair and strip your hair of its natural oils.
3. Thou shall give your hair a much needed break.
4. Thou shall keep your hair moisturized. The line of demarcation is the most fragile part of your strands and needs special attention.
5. Thou shall keep a healthy diet with plenty of water to help strength and grow hair.
6. Thou shall be patient as the hair grows out.
7. Thou shall discuss the process with family and friends.
8. Thou shall understand their hair texture and what course of action to take to transition to natural.
9. Thou shall keep ends trimmed.
10. Thou shall use a mixture consisting of water, conditioner, and oil to make it easier, less brittle, and less fragile to unravel braids.

THE SHALL NOTS FOR NATURAL

1. Thou shall not brush your hair while wet.

2. Thou shall not allow hairstyles to pull hair too tight and put pressure on strands.

3. Thou shall not dry hair with a towel. Air dry when possible.

4. Thou shall not allow stylist to pull hair too tightly. Too much pressure may weaken your hair and can result in breakage.

5. Thou shall not include all of your edges are baby hair when braiding and twisting.

6. Thou shall not oversaturate the scalp when moisturizing.

7. Thou shall not use products that are too heavy for your hair type which weighs down your afro.

8. Thou shall not use heat, especially if your hair is damaged.

9. Thou shall not rush to judgment because the process takes time.

10. Thou shall not compare your journey to someone else's transition to natural.

THE BALD MOVEMENT

WIGS, WEAVES, AND NATURAL HAIR

Models: (left to right: Erica, Nell, Nicole, and Lauren)
Photographer: Brad Phashift

When people meet Nell Coleman or view some of her modeling photographs, one of the common responses is, "She's gorgeous!" It's not because of fair skin or waist-length, flowing hair. But it's because of her chocolate skin, her warm smile and the inner beauty that pushes through to the outside despite not having a headful of hair the industry loves. In fact, her baldness helped her realize her true beauty.

After discovering her own beauty, Coleman founded The Bald Movement, which is designed to support the empowerment of people, children to elderly, to embrace the essence of being bald. Here is some of her journey of embracing the bald hairstyle and developing The Bald Movement:

"While I was in Atlanta pursuing my career as a model, I kind of became lost because I didn't know my purpose in life," said Coleman, now modeling in New York City. "What am I here for? What is it that I'm supposed to be doing to serve others? So of course in order to know your purpose in life you must know the one who created you and so I decided to go closer to God because the last thing I wanted to be was lost. So I prayed and I prayed and then along came this movement and it just made sense.

When I was younger I was bullied due to my appearance. I didn't fit in with the stereotype of beauty, and because of that I didn't love myself nor did I accept myself. So in 2010 I decided to remove the very thing that caused a lot of stress in my life and that was hair. Looking back at my life and what caused me to be bald, I decided to create this movement called, 'The Bald Movement'. With this movement, the goal was to take my past and to use that to encourage women to love themselves no matter their circumstances. The reason why I chose the bald look was because the bald look is probably one of the most unacceptable looks in the world, especially among women since hair is their glory. As such, I decided to use the bald movement to teach women that hair is not a necessity for beauty and for them to understand that true beauty is more of who you are and less of how you look. When I came to realize that, that's when I cut my hair.

I didn't really hear that I was beautiful when I had hair. I didn't really get many compliments on my beauty. I got compliments about being beautiful because of who I was. But it was crazy because once I cut my hair and became confident with myself I exuded that. When you exude confidence people can sense that. I've never in my life heard so many compliments, positive compliments, until I cut my hair. So it just seems that once I cut my hair this new me was born and I was more confident than ever and I walked with my head held high. People complimented me and I heard how beautiful I was and I don't hear a lot of negative compliments about how I look.

I have a lot of women reaching out to me saying because of this movement they are more confident, they truly understand that beauty is more than just the physical, and they believe that it's your heart and mind and soul that make you a beautiful person. I even have women with hair that tell me, 'I may not cut my hair off but you've given me a different view on life because of your movement. Your movement has helped me to be more confident even with hair. It taught me to realize that true beauty is who you are rather than how you look and it has made me stop believing that hair is my self-worth and that I am worthy regardless of how I look on the outside.' I just have a lot of people reaching out to me, thanking me for creating this movement and helping them to feel more confident with who they are.

Models: (left to right) Halaveshia, Nina, Nell, Angel, and Tanieka
Photographer: Ryan Eric

Model: Nell Coleman

Those with medical conditions

When you're diagnosed with cancer and have to do the chemo treatment, your hair falls out. You're not feeling good, the medicine has you down, and it has you weak. So what I try to tell people is that during that process a lot of women can lose their identity because they are losing their hair. So the goal is to think positive, to think highly of yourself, to do things that make you feel good and that's what I tell women who are suffering from cancer that are coming to the movement. I try to teach them to just have a positive mindset because a negative mindset can make them sicker. The way you think of yourself manifests into the universe so the goal is to stay positive and have people around you that support you, like The Bald Movement. If they don't have eyebrows or eyelashes, we show them how to put on eyebrows, how to put on eyelashes. I actually do videos where I show women how to fill in their brows so they can look and feel good. I also have this thing called 'Turban Style Thursdays' where I show women how to tie their head up in scarves and do it stylishly so that they can still feel and look cute. When you're suffering from cancer or any other disease that causes hair loss, little things like this makes a world of difference.

Keeping the movement strong

People can sense your confidence. They're like, 'OMG! You're so beautiful!' You don't even need hair to stand out. I'm not doing what everybody else is doing. I'm not wearing 27-inch long hair. I'm not conforming to European looks. I'm not doing this to be accepted by society because I'm going against the norm that's what makes me stand out. I'm choosing to say that I don't need to fit into societal standard of beauty to be accepted and moreover as long as I accept and love who I am, eventually what's going to happen is that it's going to make other people love and accept me as well. It's going to show people that you can just be yourself. And it's ok if people don't accept you because you have learned to love yourself and accept yourself. That's all that matters.

Nell's dos and donts
Do not compare yourself to others.
People are all doing it, whether we have hair, natural hair or bald head. We all compare ourselves to the next person who we feel looks better than us. Love and accept your flaws and imperfections. Love yourself just the way you are.
Find what makes you feel beautiful.
Do things that enhance your baldness.
Do things that make you feel and look your best.

Having an impact
You have people that like what the movement stands for so much that even though they aren't bald they still want to be considered bald. They want to be within this bald community because they're just loving how these women are looking and how they're truly embracing it and we literally have people who are going bald because of the movement. They see all these beautiful women on Instagram and on Facebook and its encouraging them to go back to being bald, go back to shaving their head and I think that's pretty amazing.

In five years, The Bald Movement will be working in hospitals having seminars where we will help chemo patients exude their confidence and encourage and support them. Women want to feel and look beautiful. They want to look like women and some get upset when they lose their hair. We want to visit hospitals and clinics and show them how to fill in their brows, put on lashes, put on makeup. We will have different approaches where we come together and discuss things that are going on in the world that exude a positive attitude and things that make them feel confident and beautiful. The goal is to reduce depression via classes, seminars, hospitals and clinics and help them to get back on track and feel beautiful again.

I also hope to accomplish this through fashion shows with my clothing line, Bald Apparel, which was created to help us rock our bald with purpose and style. We want to express that 'I'm a baldie, I'm proud of it, and there's nothing you can say or do to make me feel that my bald isn't beautiful.' I hope to have my apparel up and running and selling clothes and when you purchase the clothes, I put a beanie inside to give away to a child who may be going through chemo or cancer especially to keep their heads warm. It would be a cute little beanie that says 'Baldie' on it. I want to get to the point where I can send the beanies to different hospitals around the nation within five years.

www.thebaldmovement.com

Hair Loss Facts

⇒ Health issues like thyroid disease, anemia, and low vitamin levels may cause hair loss.

⇒ Alopecia areata is a disease that causes temporary hair loss in patches. It affects the hair follicles, which are part of the skin from which hairs grow. Some people get a few coin-sized patches. Others lose more hair.

⇒ Health screenings, in particular blood testing, can identify the potential for hair loss.

⇒ There are medications that can be prescribed to help with hair regrowth. Consult your dermatologist for more information.

⇒ The best way to prevent hair loss is through good nutrition, good hair hygiene, and use of the right haircare products.

⇒ Iron levels and the amount of vitamin B in your body are important to hair loss and prevention of hair loss.

⇒ Stress is a major contributor to hair loss.

⇒ Multivitamins that include vitamin B, iron, folate, zinc and calcium have been recommended to help prevent hair loss and stimulate growth. Biotin and vitamin B12 have also been known to help hair growth.

Hair loss clients:

In addition to working with models, celebrities and other high profile clients, Stylist Egypt Buck works with hair loss clients. He said it's personal to him knowing that he not only helps women look good but feel good. "A lot of time they feel that they can't look or feel beautiful because they lost their hair. Sometimes wigs don't work or they don't fit the way people want them to. Or they've gone through injections, creams, powders, and have tried hair clubs, and nothing is working to bring the hair back. We consult with them to see what's best for them and we make handmade pieces with human hair and we teach them about upkeep. The process can be very emotional. You have to be willing to take care of it. And they look good and you can see when they start feeling better about themselves."

HEALTHIER HAIR WITH GIOVAN LANE

THC spoke to Giovan Lane, founder and product designer for cinagrOrganic Healthy Hair Products, about her experience going natural and developing her products. A senior scientist at a pharmaceutical company, is passionate about educating on natural haircare not just products. Here is what she said about the genesis of her journey:

I entrusted my hair to someone who was supposed to be a professional and I had a bad experience. She burned my hair by using a flat iron that was too hot. As a result I had to cut my hair off because it was crispy and crunchy. It was horrible and thin so I just cut it off. From there I started utilizing my research capabilities to see what I can do to make my hair grow and make it grow healthy.

Through my research, I automatically knew that I wanted to stop using relaxers and go natural. Even though I am in the science field I didn't consider what I was doing to my hair, my curl patterns and changing the texture of it by using lye-based relaxers. So I just stopped relaxing my hair and I started going towards the natural hair movement and it was prior to this craze of the natural hair movement. I educated myself about what happens when you apply these harsh chemicals.

I played around with natural certified organic herbs, certified organic oils, and learned what they do and what their key benefits were when you implement them into your haircare regimen. As a result, I started incorporating them into my haircare regimen. I saw some really positive improvements in my hair and what it was doing. I didn't start my company, but that's where the story began. When I started, it was just to get my hair back in good health and it snowballed into going the more natural route. My family and my friends started seeing my hair improve and looking healthier and they wanted to know what my secret was, what I was doing. So I said try some of this oil and see what happens. I gave them some samples and they started seeing differences in their hair. Their hair was healthy and they told me, 'G, you're onto something. You really should get this out there and help everybody get the benefits of using this herbal concoction.

From there I started researching how to open a business, how to form a limited liability company, what I would name my product line amongst other things. It just took on a mind of its own.

When I went to college for biology, I wanted to be a doctor. I had no inkling that I would have anything to do with the haircare industry. My parents are highly involved in the haircare industry and have been for basically my whole life. My mom is a hair care professional. My stepfather has a national magazine like a directory for barber shops and salons called National Solid Gold so we were always at the hair shows and I would help with the family selling books. So I was accustomed to being around the hair care industry, but I never saw biology and the hair industry meeting. But now I know this is my calling and now I see both worlds meeting and its really wild being there.

Giovan Lane, Founder cinagrOrganic
Photo by: Carlos Payne/National Solid Gold

THC: How long did it take to start seeing results?

Lane: It started in 2007 when my hair started getting 'crispy' and I had to figure out what to do with my hair. It wasn't from day one that it was the perfect concoction so I had to do trial and error to get to the point where I am now. At first I was walking around looking like a grizzly bear and it just wasn't working for me. I was like 'No this is not the bomb. Oh no!' I just had to figure it out on my own and that's how I was able to use my research background. If I didn't have that I don't know how I would've dealt with it. I was tweaking and trying to reformulate and come up with the perfect combination to get to the final product.

THC: At what point did you start seeing the results that were consistent enough to start the company?

Lane: I didn't start the company until 2011. It was just one product initially and then from there people were asking about shampoos, and conditioner. So I decided to accommodate their demands, I had to extend the offering so that people would buy the products and in turn by the entire line, because that's what they were looking for. They saw the benefits of what the oil was doing and then I came out with a vitamin moisturizer that you can use on the entire strand of the hair and it's not as weighty as the oil. It had a more instantaneous reaction to it. For example if somebody started using the oil they would start seeing growth within three weeks but it depends on their consistency and their commitment to their healthy hair movement. If they are not going to remain committed and use the product as they should or as directed then it's not going to work. A lot of people don't understand or fully grasp the concept of hair growth and obtaining healthy hair because they have microwave mentality. They are the type of people that will put a weave on their head or braid their hair than to really commit themselves to obtaining healthy hair and that's basically what I'm trying to change.

In our community, a lot of us as black people want things and want things now and we take the easy way out when it comes to our hair. Some people go to a store and buy an 8-inch pack of weave and glue it to their head instead of buying my little $20 bottle or $12 bottle oil. If you use that you can get the eight inches that you just bought. But it's just the mentality. It's very skewed when it comes to hair.

THC: When did you start seeing this whole national hair movement and you seeing that more people are taking better care of their hair because of it?

Lane: I think it's awesome how the movement has taken on a mind of its own. Just going online and seeing the growth of these bloggers who are just really regular people, initially it started with forums, there was one that I followed religiously when I was just starting my transition from relaxed to natural. There were some key females that started their 'You tube Channels' who people follow religiously; they are put up on a pedestal so much so that they are actually celebrities, they are being endorsed by private companies, they're making money and living just from being subject matter experts in the natural hair movement. It's just amazing to me how it went from 0-100 overnight, because of the fact that social media is so powerful and it shows how powerful social media is.

"I think it's awesome how the (natural hair) movement has taken on a mind of its own."

Giovan Lane

THC: Where will the natural hair movement be in say five years?

Lane: I was just talking to my girlfriend about this today and she asked me, 'Do you think we're going to go back to relying on perming our hair with relaxers?' I think over the course of time we will see a decline in the buying of weaves because I think that people will start to wear their own hair now celebrities are showing that they feel good in their own skin being natural. We've also seen a decline in the market of relaxers. I don't know the exact figures but I know there is a definite decline in the industry of relaxers.

It's a powerful thing. I think that if they haven't already done so almost everyone is considering going natural and going back to our roots. What's happening is they're seeing how versatile natural hair can be. Back in the day when people would say, 'Oh my hair is natural,' you'd think they were wearing an afro or just kinky. But now people that are natural are wearing their hair straight, they're wearing it curly, or kinky. There are so many different styles but it's their hair. I think people are embracing that.

THC: For people who are on the fence and are considering going natural, what show they know?

Lane: I think they should consider what they're doing to themselves, what they're doing to the environment, and the image that they are portraying to their children. I had friends that were relaxing their hair until they had daughters and they went natural instantly because they didn't want their daughters to have the wrong view of what was pretty was or that beautiful long flowing hair is the only pretty hair. They wanted to give their daughters a positive image of what being beautiful was. A lot of the magazines are showing what they think is beautiful as being somebody with straight hair and somebody with make up on, all this fake stuff.

THC: What tips do you have for people with natural hair?
Lane: I think with your hair and with your body, people should take heed to what their body is really telling them. If you're putting something in your body or on your body that's wrong, your body is going to telling you this is toxic, stop doing that or else. So I think that people should be more vigilant as to what their body is telling them and what their hair is telling them. For example if your messing with your hair too much and its snapping off, you need to see what you're doing wrong, what products are you using that you should stop. People will always come to me and say, 'My hair is breaking off. I don't know what's going on.' I ask them, 'How often do you use heat in your hair?' or "Are you using too much protein?' If you use too much protein in your hair, it's going to build up and cause it to snap and break. So you have to have a healthy balance of moisture and protein in your haircare regimen. I would advise them that if they have to have heat in their hair only do it on freshly washed hair. Do not put heat on hair that is not freshly washed because you're just burning your hair.

Giovan Lane, founder of cinagrOrganic
www.cinagrOrganic.com

ANCIENT SECRETS WITH TEMEKA ROYSTER

The hair products at Ancient Secrets Beauty, including the bestselling hair growth oil, shampoo, detangler, and five different conditioners, are created predominately for ethnic hair. The oil helps moisturize the hair, softens the texture, and accelerates the growth of the hair usually starting in 2-3 weeks. I created the product about seven years ago but I just never told anybody about it. That's why I called it an ancient secret. Some of the ingredients have been used since Egyptian times in 2000 B.C. So they are very old, organic ingredients. Basically the recipe came to me in a dream. I started keeping a dream journal right next to my bed and when I woke up, I wrote down all the ingredients and what it was according to that dream. Then I started studying it and doing holistic therapy. I got a certification in holistic therapy. Then I started using the oil on myself and then released it to the public about two and a half years ago.

The ingredients include lemon grass, lavender and other oils to break it down. They are all natural. I probably noticed growth in about two weeks. I also noticed a better shine. The texture was softer. People used to say, 'You have beautiful hair' or they would say, 'Your hair is so long.' Whenever I would go to a stylist to get my hair done, everybody would glance over because it was that stigma that African American women couldn't grow hair. Most women in there who had lengthy hair were wearing weave. Well of course I don't believe that stereotype. You can grow your own hair. But some women were just impressed. They kept asking me how I got my hair like that so I started telling people about it. But for a long time I didn't mention it. I guess they thought it was just genetics.

I was home on medically leave. I was home for three months. I kind of got tired of staring at the wall. I would get on the computer, journal and write. I was on Facebook and I was in a forum and we were talking about hair and I said I don't use anybody's oil on my head but my own. Another lady said where do you get this oil from? I said I haven't really sold it to anyone, it's just my personal oil. She said she wanted to try it. So I said if you are serious, I'll send you an invoice. I sent her one and another lady said I want one too. I sent her one and the word started getting around so I said I better start putting up some sort of website or something because maybe they like it. From there, it grew to where I quit my job in like a year and a half and I had been working in the criminal justice field for 14 years. I worked my way up, right under the warden as a program director. I was able to quit my job. It's really been a blessing.

"You have to start with appreciating the hair that you have."
Temeka Royster

Temeka's Two Biggest Shalls

- **Love the hair that God gave you.** Sometimes we look at other people's hair and say, 'If only I had her hair or I wish I had hair like that.' You have to start with appreciating the hair that you have. There are women who can take their hair and make wonderful styles. Just like the afros are coming back, the naturals are coming back. Work with what you were given. Some people love weave more than their own hair. They spend $300 on weave but won't spend $10 to nurture their own hair. But when you take your hair down, it's broken off or it's not growing because you're not taking care of it and you put it right back up. You have to love what you have first.

- **Be patient.** Hair grows from the root but is retained from the end. If your ends are split or damaged, it's not going to show a lot of growth because it's growing from the root but falling out on the end. You have to do a thorough check of your hair just like when you take your car to the mechanic and they do a diagnosis.

Temeka Royster, founder of Ancient Secrets Beauty products

www.blackhairgrowth.biz

HAIRNAMICS HAIR VITAMINS WITH KIM KEARNEY

Kim Kearney, director of marketing for Hairnamics, a new hair vitamin with a combination of biotin and iron to produce longer, stronger and healthier hair, shared her experience and tips for natural hair:

Being an African-American female, I was really excited to even discover my own natural hair. Most of us went through the childhood phase of having our hair pressed out and in our teenage and young adult years we jumped to the relaxer as soon as we could, not realizing the damage it does to our hair. Most of us are addicted to weaving and extensions among other things because we want the long locks, we want the long flashy flowing hair and we were brainwashed to think that we couldn't grow our own hair. But the truth is our own hair will grow. I was even taken aback when I finally let the relaxer grow out and discovered that I had really thick curly hair. I never knew that. All I remember was my hair being pressed out as a kid. I went to visit some family members a year or so ago and I wore my own hair and they were looking at me like, 'Baby do you need me to press that out for you?' They thought I was crazy for wearing my own natural hair but I loved it. It's like a kinky curly texture and I am just excited for the whole natural hair movement.

People think you have long hair because it is in your genes. Yes, genes play a role but nutrition has a lot to do with it. What we consume and what's on the inside have a lot to do with what we see on the outside. So the beauty of

Hairnamics is that they have really gotten into the science of great hair and they have come up with an amazing hair vitamin formula that includes iron. I have tried other hair vitamins and usually a lot of people talk about this online and their reviews are that some of the other vitamins have caused side effects like their skin breaks out or they end up with a lot of shedding, especially if they stop using the vitamin. Hairnamics does not have those side effects they took all the ingredients that causes those issues and we haven't had any complaints about side effects.

This vitamin has what is called the iron balance, 3000 mcg of iron and 3000 mcg of biotin along with a total of 29 key ingredients. The importance of iron being incorporated is that most African Americans are iron deficient. I went for a check-up and the physician asked me, 'Is your skin dry? Is your hair normally dry? Are your nails brittle?' And I was like, 'Yes, why?' I was concerned. He said because you have low iron. Women of African descent tend to be more iron deficient and this is why our hair is normally dry, this is why we have so much breakage and we're susceptible to damage from hot styles and heat styles and curlers and blow dryers and the chemical treatment. Everybody wants the Beyoncé look. I did it too and went blonde and right now Hairnamics is saving my hair. I thought I would have to do a big chop and start all over because of the damage from the blonde.

We really need to realize that what you put in your body certainly affects the results you get on the outside. It affects your skin and definitely affects your hair and your nails. That iron component has made a tremendous stride in helping us to grow this brand. The first time we came out a few months ago, we sold out when we launched because women recognized that they have low iron too. Some people have recorded that they have gotten more energy and they're working out now. It's really having a positive effect on people. They are noticing the difference in their skin. They have more elasticity, they're not having breakouts, they're having more vibrant skin, and they look more youthful. And there is hair growth.

My hair grew over three and a half inches in two and a half weeks which was like a miracle because my hair only grew an eighth of an inch each month. So to have more than double the hair growth taking this vitamin has been amazing results for me. We have been getting so many great responses and not just from women. Now we have men who have contacted us and are now using the products because some guys want longer hair since they're trying to dread or they want braids or their hair is thin. It's just an amazing product that can work across the board. So you can put all that curly pudding and castor oil, argon oil, Moroccan oil and all these treatments and all the conditioners on your hair on the outside but if you don't nurture your hair from the inside, you are not going to have strong, healthy hair.

Kim's tips:
- Care for your hair from the inside out.
- Keep your hair moisturized.
- Avoid products that are alcohol-based.
- Avoid heat in your hair.
- Keep your ends trimmed.
- Avoid hair color and other chemicals.
- Don't let your stylist braid too tight.

www.hairnamics.com

STYLISTS SOUNDOFF

ANGELA STUCKEY
EGYPT BUCK
SHIZZ
SABINE HENDERSON
ARLAND D. HOWARD
JAI PROCTOR
LAURRIN
ANGELA GRAY
DANA ROXETTE
SHAWNESE MCDANIEL
SHAKIRA V. CLARK
TENEL DORSEY
TONI CHAPMAN

Angela Stuckey, owner of Shadez of Beauty in Chesapeake, Virginia, is an award-winning stylist with more than 30 national competition recognitions to her credit, including best stylist, weave artist of the year, fantasy hair competition winner, and overall #1 stylist at The Bronner Brothers Hair Show in Atlanta.

"I've been in the salon industry since 12," she said. "I always knew that I had a gift in hair. I was one of the kids that always had dolls and did their hair. I used to do my mom's hair and her friends' hair. I opened my first salon when I was 22."

Angela is not surprised by the recent changes in the hair and haircare industry and said people can expect to see even more changes in years to come.

"Hair and haircare are always changing. Right now weave is the thing. Everybody can do (weave). Everybody can YouTube it. In five years, weave will take over if stylists don't educate themselves."

She said you can't get certain products anymore because people don't care about their hair anymore. "All they want is weave. At hair shows, instead of there being as many products to strengthen and grow hair, weave companies are more visible with their products. But that's going to hurt consumers who don't care for their hair in the long run. So consumers need to be educated on their hair as well as stylist need to be educated on the changes in haircare products and services so they can educate their clients. You have to maintain your natural hair."

New York City freelance stylist Egypt Buck echoed those sentiments after witnessing the weave craze and the natural hair movement growing.

"Stylists have to be proactive to make sure they know what's going on with the changes in the industry," said Egypt, who works for a hair replacement salon that builds custom hair pieces for clients with alopecia, cancer and other hair loss conditions. "They have to educate their clients about what helps and harms their hair."

For example, he said people need to know that just because their hair is braided, it doesn't mean that it's growing. They still have to take care of their own hair. A lot of people don't realize their hair has to rest and they have to keep their scalps healthy for healthy hair.

Egypt's Top Tips:
- Always have your ends trimmed regardless of the style.
- Everything isn't meant for everybody.
- You need a professional to prevent hair issues, address bad hair situations, and to work with you through your changing hair styles.

Model: Sheila J   **Photographer:** Nay Marie

Courtesy of Egypt Buck/Nay Marie Photography

Stylist SHIZZ, Glam Elite Enterprise

"I have been in this industry for many years which has allowed me to not only build a global name for myself but it has also allowed me to shift the rules, break down boundaries and create new measures. One of the greatest things I love about the industry at this time is the unity and networking that has been reintroduced to the world of hair, fashion, barbering and styling.

Tips: 1. Always use hair serums and heat protectants when getting a styling session. 2. When getting any hair extension installed be sure that your installer treats your natural hair prior to the install. Never put hair extensions on poor, weak or fragile hair. Your hair must be as healthy as possible before going into being covered for months at a time.

Stylist Sabine Henderson, Universal Designz Salon, Mableton, GA

"I've noticed that when ladies put extensions in their hair, they don't shampoo it regularly. I would suggest they visit their stylist once a week to get the extensions shampooed and treated as you would your natural hair."

"I've seen a lot of bloggers say that pressing combs cause heat damage. That's a myth. The pressing comb does not take away your curl pattern. The curl pattern is just relaxed. If you keep the heat out of your hair for a couple months the pattern will revert to its natural curl pattern."

Stylist Arland D. Howard, Anointed Hands Hair Care, Pittsburgh, PA.

"I am a beautician not a magician. You are a human not a plant. Dirt does not make your hair grow."

Tips:
- Ends should be trimmed every six weeks.
- Do not relax little girls' hair under the age of 12 even if the box has a little girl on it. It's still chemicals.

Stylist Jai Proctor, Studio J. Salon, Pittsburgh, PA

As a professional, I feel that it is very important to take care of your "own" hair. It's all right to wear extensions, braids, etc., but most importantly your hair should be cared for while in these styles. I find that some leave in their sew-ins way too long, as long as 3-4 months. Some even up to six months. Eight to 10 weeks should be the maximum.

If you want to reuse the hair because you paid a lot for it, take it out to be cleaned properly by a professional and reinstalled. I've also noticed a lot of stylists or "unlicensed" stylists put too much tension on the hair when braiding and weaving. This only weakens the hair, causes breakage, can cause hair loss and even alopecia. Lastly, the hair/beauty industry is flooded with people who aren't licensed and promote videos all over YouTube for even more unlicensed professionals to try it out. Some of them are pretty good but there are those who don't know the damage they may be causing and teaching others. If you need to look something up, go to a licensed professional's site/channel where they know what they're talking about. Most importantly go see a professional stylist. Everything shouldn't be done at home. Love your hair with the proper care.

Stylist Laurrin, Xxposurhair by Laurrin, Atlanta, GA
Here are a few tips:
- Cleanse hair weekly (natural and relaxed)
- Caucasian hair should be cleansed daily if it produces a lot of oil
- Use shampoos that treat the scalp, not just the hair
- Cocktail oil/silk to your conditioner for more moisture & deeper penetrates
- If you're looking for a new stylist ask questions to make sure he/she meets your needs
- Suggested products: S-Factor, Shea Moisture, CHI, Jane Carter solutions, Kera-Care, Basic.

Stylist Angela Gray, Deniya's Beauty Salon, Baltimore, Maryland
"Most people (black women) are reverting back to their natural roots, their natural hair and embracing what is a part of their culture."
- Tip: Return to the salons. Stop taking shortcuts because you'll only get black market hair care. You pay for what you get so get professional licensed treatment.

Stylist Dana Roxette   **Photo by:** Sean Cokes

Stylist Dana Roxette, Hairrox, College Park, GA

"We are currently living in a billion dollar hair era, from thousands of natural hair products on shelves or tons of hair extension shipments crossing the seas. Some consider it the best of both worlds, embracing and flaunting what was genetically given or protecting the hair with extensions, when installed properly. We have become an adventurous generation with eclectic styles on YouTube while at home keeping edgy and classic looks. The common denominator is maintaining healthy hair. To do this one must select proper clarifiers, hydrators, and professionals to deliver the proper services. A regular trimming of your ends, styling products with low alcohol content, and low maintenance every day will create the healthy tresses desired. Consult a professional to determine what's best for you and your lifestyle."

Stylist Shawnese McDaniel, Muse Salon and Spa, Johns Creek, GA

"Even though sew-in hair extensions, braids and other protective styles are becoming more and more popular, keep in mind nothing makes your hair grow healthier than the right haircare regimen. Here are a few tips to keep your hair happy:

- Use the recommended hair products by your local stylist. This can prevent breakage and dry split ends. Sometimes overuse, underuse and misuse of products can cause a lack of good results on your hair.
- Keep your ends trimmed regularly (usually every 8-10 weeks.)
- Deep conditioning treatments are mandatory. This adds a much needed boost to your hair giving it strength and moisture.
- Make sure you take breaks in between your protective styles. This prevents the weakening of the edges of your hair as wells as hair loss from excessive pulling.
- Remember too much of anything isn't good. Do everything in moderation and with your professional stylists suggestions you and your hair will have happy results.

Stylist Shakira V. Clark
Photo by: Glenn Parson Photography

Stylist Shakira V. Clark, Atlanta, GA

Healthy hair begins with a healthy lifestyle. Before we get to the outside, we need to take care of the inside. What you eat, drink and how you treat your body has an effect on your hair. You need to eat enough fresh fruits and vegetables, drink enough water and exercise regularly for your body's overall health.

Get longer, beautiful, healthier hair by making these changes. It's a lifestyle.

- Regular trims are necessary!

This sounds counterproductive if you want your hair to grow longer, but trims help get rid of dry, damaged and split ends which can work their way up the shaft of your hair, causing even more damage. A trim is defined as removing ¼ to ½-inch of hair, nothing more. If your stylist insists on cutting off inches every time you go in for a visit, your hair won't get longer and instead of a trim, it becomes a haircut!

- Use the right tools!

Silk or Satin Hair Cover - At night a hair scarf/bonnet or even a silk or satin pillowcase will go a long way toward retaining moisture in the hair and having a longer lasting hairstyle.

- Use the proper hot tools!

Additional heat on the hair should be a bare minimal and simply used for touch ups to the hair. When you are using a hot tool element, it's important to know the what type of heating tool is best for your hair. Titanium flat irons may be a little costly but they are well worth it when it comes to long-lasting health with your hair.

Stylist Tenel Dorsey, Dreamz Hair Salon, Pittsburgh, PA

"Always remember healthy hair starts from within. Eat your veggies and vitamins to give your hair the luster and growth it needs. Don't allow product pushers and society to make you buy miracle products, hoping for a magic trick. Start with your own knowledge and abilities or call Dreamz."

Stylist Toni Chapman, Studio 22, South Carolina.

"Every night massage your scalp with fingertips or brush for a minute or two. This stimulates hair growth."

WRAP UP

Having choices about how you wear your hair is liberating. Finding what works best for you may take time, effort, money, and patience but it is worth it. The healthier you keep your scalp and hair the more choices you will have from wigs to weaves to naturals. It is a good idea to keep a hair journal and write in it as often as you feel but at least once a week. This will help you remember and understand what works best for your hair. For each journal entry include the following:

1. The date
2. Measure your hair from root to end at the nape, in the middle, on each side, and the front
3. Include a photo or description
4. Who styled it
5. What was used
6. How you feel about it

We have included a few blank pages at the end of the book for note-taking and to get you started with your journal. Create an online journal as well. They are great because you can upload photos to track your progress and share your process on blogs and social media.

Be certain to follow us on social media and look out for more from **#TheHairCommandments #THC**.

Get to know your hair, learn what it needs, try new things, and have fun.

#TheHairCommandments #THC

Get to know your hair, learn what it needs, try new things, and have fun.

#TheHairCommandments   #THC

THE HAIR COMMANDMENTS

Get to know your hair, learn what it needs, try new things, and have fun.

#TheHairCommandments #THC

WIGS, WEAVES, AND NATURAL HAIR

Get to know your hair, learn what it needs, try new things, and have fun.

#TheHairCommandments   #THC

ABOUT THE AUTHORS

LaToya Johnson-Rainey is owner of A Hair Boutique in Pittsburgh, PA, which sells high-end wigs and hair products. The shop's mission is Just Be Beautiful: Restoring Confidence & Empowering Women. After working five years with her family's beauty supply business, Johnson-Rainey realized there was a niche for an intimate place where women could shop for wigs, be comfortable, and learn about wig care & maintenance from someone compassionate. Johnson-Rainey, who earned her MBA in business innovation and administration from Carlow University, has spent countless hours researching hair, trends, and hair products. She is quickly becoming one of the foremost experts in the ever-growing hair and hair care industry and is the featured speaker for Just Be Beautiful seminars at various organizations.

C. Nathaniel Brown is a bestselling author, publisher, and writing coach. He is author of five other successful books, including Making Wings; Xs, Os, and Ws; and The Business of My Book, which assists his goal of helping 10,000 writers publish. He is also a motivational and inspirational speaker on topics such as writing and publishing; living your dreams; turning your passion into your profession; and overcoming obstacles to success. He also hosts the popular radio program, The C. Nathaniel Brown Show which is based in Atlanta where he resides.

WE WELCOME YOUR COMMENTS, QUESTIONS AND REVIEWS OF THE HAIR COMMANDMENTS. SHARE YOUR THOUGHTS AND OPINIONS AT:
EXPECTEDENDENTERTAINMENT@GMAIL.COM
WWW.AMAZON.COM

ALSO SHARE YOUR THOUGHTS ON SOCIAL MEDIA USING THE HASHTAGS
#THEHAIRCOMMANDMENTS
#THC
WWW.FACEBOOK.COM/THEHAIRCOMMANDMENTS
WWW.THEHAIRCOMMANDMENTS.COM

FOR MORE TITLES FROM EX3 BOOKS

VISIT OUR WEBSITE AT:
www.EX3ent.com

CPSIA information can be obtained
at www.ICGtesting.com
Printed in the USA
FFOW03n1405220317
33777FF